Helping in Social Work

By the same author

Client-Worker Transactions
Freedom and the Welfare State
Paupers: The Making of the New Claiming Class
Poor Parents: Social Policy and the Cycle of Deprivation
The Social Worker in Family Situations

Helping in Social Work

Bill Jordan

Department of Sociology
University of Exeter

Routledge & Kegan Paul
London, Boston and Henley

First published in 1979
by Routledge & Kegan Paul Ltd
39 Store Street, London WC1E 7DD,
Broadway House, Newtown Road,
Henley-on-Thames, Oxon RG9 1EN and
9 Park Street, Boston, Mass. 02108, USA
Set in 11 on 12pt IBM Baskerville
and printed in Great Britain by
Caledonian Graphics Ltd

British Library Cataloguing in Publication Data

Jordan, Bill

Helping in social work.
1. Social service
I. Title
361 HV40 78-41008

ISBN 0 7100 0126 6
ISBN 0 7100 0127 4 Pbk

Contents

Preface

Some of my friends have read this book in typescript, and suggested that I should preface it with a brief warning to my readers. Many of the examples I have given are reproduced without much comment and analysis of why I said or did what I did. They are raw accounts of events, and reflect my own personal style of trying to help people in distress. They would not necessarily work for others, and are not presented as a model to be copied. As I have tried to explain throughout the book, I believe each social worker must try to evolve his own style and methods, and make them true to himself.

1 The helper

It sounds simpleminded to talk of social work as 'helping people'; yet it is difficult to find a better way of describing what social workers try to do. To 'intervene' or 'monitor' may seem more professional, but after any amount of intervention and monitoring it is still reasonable to ask, 'Did it help?' Whether or not a social worker is helpful often appears to depend on a personal process of communication and influence.

This is only one aspect of what social work is, but it is a sufficiently important and difficult one to deserve attention in its own right. To the man in the street, nothing could be more obvious than that people in trouble are often hard to help, and that people who help them need special qualities and strengths. Yet surprisingly little has been written recently about the personal processes of influence in social work – the effects, for better or worse, that social workers and clients have on each other in their face-to-face encounters.

There are many reasons for this. The vast majority of social workers are now employed by state agencies to deal with social problems which have been officially recognised as requiring some public remedy. Such agencies are part of the network of institutions which make provision for large-scale human problems. The methods which the state uses to combat many social evils are relatively impersonal, based on measurement, planning and organisation. Social work agencies themselves have become large and complex. Thus the average social worker is a member of the social services department of a municipality which employs a staff of hundreds of others like himself. From one point of view, what he does can be seen in terms of implementing statutory regulations and allocating certain resources between needy members of the community.

So there is something of a paradox. The scale of human problems in our society has led to large social work organisations, but the day-to-day business of these departments is still small-scale, humble, and determined by the personal influence of social workers and clients on each other. Good planning and policies can only be made effective through good practice. This cannot be learnt by procedures or rules of thumb. Helping people requires different skills from framing strategies for overcoming social problems.

Much recent writing about social work has been confined to organisational studies and discussion of the structure and priorities of agencies. In reaction against this, some writers have attempted to refocus attention on the personal and qualitative elements in social work, and to describe new methods of helping people. Unfortunately, these latter writings have tended to be fragmented between a number of rather esoteric therapeutic schools. Each school has its own philosophical, ethical or scientific basis, its own terminology (often obscure) and its own (often mystifying) technical apparatus. Some of them give the appearance of operating as exclusive sects, and many imply that their morals and their methods are incompatible with all or most of the tasks performed by statutory social workers. The result is an impression that social workers employed by the local authority or the probation service are no more than municipal officials or civil servants, and that anyone who really wants to help people should seek employment in the private sector – in a voluntary agency, or in some highly specialised facility which caters for the needs of the bizarrely afflicted and those who can afford its fees.

I do not agree with this conclusion. My aim in this book is to write a simple, practical and positive account of what I see as the elements which could make up good practice in the sort of work which statutory social workers do. I want if possible to avoid using the jargons of either the organisational theories of official social work, or the therapeutic schools. In order to achieve this simplicity, I shall try to avoid references to other writings and quotations from other authors. However, it should be perfectly clear to the reader that I am relying heavily both on much that is well established in the literature of social work, and on many newer ideas and techniques from a number of sources.

In writing it, I started out to expound certain theories. Having tried to do this, I found that there was something very unsatisfactory about the result. In nearly every case, the ideas I was trying to convey were better contained and illustrated in the experience on which they were based. So I have completely rewritten it, cutting out much of the argument and analysis, and concentrating on giving examples from practice.

Of necessity, any such account is a very personal one, and draws heavily on thirteen years of experience, first as a probation officer, and more recently as a social worker in a mental hospital. But it also draws on lessons that I have learnt from teaching social work students and visting them in placements in other settings, particularly in social services departments.

Very often, accounts of social work practice start with some discussion of the motives, values and attitudes that social workers need to have in order to help their clients. This usually ends in a list of rather high-sounding principles. I doubt whether these principles are particularly useful for people who want to improve their capacity to help. They tend to be very abstract, and hence difficult to apply. I suspect that our real motives and attitudes, the ones that most affect what we actually do as social workers, are derived from experiences of helping and being helped. These are processes we have all undergone in everyday life, and which we have used in our attempts to develop a method of working with clients. We may well want to generalise about these experiences, and to call these generalisations 'principles'. But we are unlikely to be able to understand what exactly someone else means by his generalisations unless he can specify some of the experiences which led to them, or unless we are sufficiently familiar with his practice in specific cases to see what he actually does. We can learn from others, but only by understanding their experiences, and through them re-examining our own.

When I was a very young and new probation officer, I had a much wiser and older colleague who often used to say, apparently in any and every context, 'The best thing is to do nothing'. I found this mystifying and infuriating, and at first I got no help from it. I had no notion how it looked or felt to do nothing – the mechanics of this masterly inactivity. As I got to know him better and to see him in action, I began to realise what he meant. I myself would not even have chosen those words to describe his imperturbable survival of his clients' crises, his calm willingness to stick with them, or his refusal to be panicked into pointless busy doing. But once I saw for myself I not only understood, but was able to use his 'principle' in my own work, to correct my sometimes restless over-anxiety to be helpful. I suspect that similarly our lack of detailed knowledge of the content and context of such principles as 'acceptance', 'non-judgmentalism' and 'confidentiality' makes them equally hard to apply.

So I intend instead to start this book with an attempt to trace my own origins as a social worker, and more particularly how I came to have the beliefs about and attitudes towards helping that I now hold. This necessarily means that I have to trace my own personal history back to fairly early experiences of people I found helpful or unhelpful, of being helped, and of starting to try to help others. I must apologise in advance if this exercise sounds self-indulgent. I feel it is a necessary introduction to what I have to say about helping in social work, without which the rest of the book would be incomplete and even possibly misleading.

For it is an important part of how I understand the process of helping in social work that it is not essentially different from certain other kinds of help people give each other; and that to be effective it demands the use of the helper's whole personality, not just a professional segment of it. Thus it is quite inappropriate for me to generalise or pontificate about what values and attitudes social workers ought to have. It is much more relevant to trace those I now hold, as a key to understanding the kind of social work practice I shall later describe. I shall try to select experiences which seem to have influenced my development as a helper, and to spare the reader a detailed history of other aspects of my life.

First of all, it is probably worth mentioning that I spent part of my childhood in South Africa. In this may well lie the origins of my identification with the underdog and the oppressed, which I shall mention again later in this chapter. But it also partly explains a fundamental ambivalence about receiving help which I had throughout my early years. It was part of the rugged and philistine culture of such a boyhood that needing help with anything was a sign of weakness, and that having feelings about anything indicated a quite dangerous softness. I had strong reservations about the values of this culture, but I was also a coward about expressing these reservations in words or action. I played games, fought and suppressed my emotions with the best of them, never wanting to appear different, yet secretly refusing to identify with those I imitated.

I was quite often aware that this culture was limiting, uncreative and even brutal. But I was much less conscious of the positive value of sharing feelings and emotional closeness. During this period (when I was aged between five and thirteen) I think I carried over some of the reserve and self-control I learnt at school into my relations with my family. I neither sought nor expected understanding of what I felt, and was content to guess at the feelings of others.

So it was only in flashes that, in early adolescence, I began to experience the value of what I can best describe as communication between the 'middle' of one person and the 'middle' of another. One incident stands out in my memory. When I was about twelve, my parents separated. My father used to visit on Sundays, and take me to play cricket with him at my grandfather's house nearby. For several weeks in succession I remember batting in a style that was quite unlike my normal one. My father's bowling was gentle and inviting, but I played back to every ball and poked it defensively in the direction of gulley. My father said nothing about these dismal performances, and I attributed them to a sensation of sickness that always seemed to accompany my dreary innings. One day I was walking home with him, with a feeling of heaviness and distance between us, when he said, quietly and without looking at me, that he realised that I must be angry with him and hurt that he had left home, and probably this was why I was batting so defensively. My first instinct was to deny this, and I think I did. But the remark struck me very strongly, partly because my father seldom said such things, but also because its effect on me seemed to indicate that it was true and important. It made a sort of sense of what had previously been muddled, uncomfortable, meaningless and somehow all knotted-up inside me. I felt grateful that he had been able to say it. It was as if this truth between us, however painful, released something in me, and allowed me to feel closer to him.

Before this I had more or less assumed that it was a good thing to suppress emotions and ride out personal discomfort as if it was a storm that would pass. That had seemed the only sensible and dignified way to behave – to make as little fuss as possible, and wait for bad feelings to go away. Self-discipline and toughness were the opposites of softness, which meant giving in to one's emotions. But then it began to dawn on me for the first time that there might possibly be an even more demanding discipline which required that I was true to my own feelings and to other people's, and that this might ultimately be much more satisfying. Instead of being self-sufficient, it might be better to be in contact with the central parts of others' experiences and personalities, and perhaps even to let them be in contact with mine. I still felt very ambivalent about this glimpse of another world that I had been given, but it was important. For what I had experienced was that in an everyday situation there were certain essentials in people's immediate feelings about each other which in themselves constituted some kind of truths, and that if these could be reached and shared, it helped, even if the feelings were painful. Even the acknowledgment and sharing of pain had been helpful.

Another aspect of this experience was that the communication had been a good in itself. I could recognise and value it as significant, even though there were no obvious consequences. Nothing special happened between myself and my father as a result of his reaching the middle of me. There was no great new 'bond' or 'breakthrough'. Shortly afterwards, I and the rest of the family moved away from South Africa, and he stayed. I have only seen him briefly twice in the past twenty-odd years. But that moment meant something to me at the time, and has stayed with me throughout the intervening years.

During my adolescence, the notion of getting nearer to other people and being more open and truthful about feelings impressed me increasingly, but much more as an ideal than in reality. I still found self-revelation very difficult. This may have had something to do with the small-town community in which I spent this part of my life. Everyone knew each other so well through a daily round of contacts that little needed to be explained or made explicit. Indeed, a degree of reserve seemed necessary for the growth of a separate and independent identity. It was only when I left home for the first time to go to university that I realised how much I had come to rely on that strong sense of knowing others and being known by them. I felt a sudden need to be acknowledged and recognised, with all my weaknesses, by the strangers amongst whom I was now living, and this urge occasionally overwhelmed my instincts for self-concealment. In one case, I presented to someone I had only very recently met a short autobiography under the title 'Confessions of an Intellectual Corpse', which I insisted he read before deciding whether to cultivate my acquaintance any further.

Yet I was aware of how far from the ideal of truth-to-feelings such gestures were. It was easy, both at home and at university, to spot in myself and others where we stopped short of honesty and realism. Under the guise of confiding or sharing, we would attempt to justify ourselves or elicit sympathy. In the way we presented ourselves to each other, we would try to emphasise our importance or assuage our guilt. Some of us overdramatised ourselves and our emotions; others (myself especially) adopted a self-mocking tone that deflected both criticism and closeness. All this was, of course, a very necessary part of being young, and for the vast majority of the time I was delighted to enjoy being frivolous and superficial. But a serious-minded bit of me was aware that even when we pretended to try, we very seldom communicated between the middles of ourselves.

Indeed it sometimes struck me that if that ideal could not be achieved, perhaps it was better for people not to go through the pretence of attempting it. Hearing people 'talking about problems' without any real commitment or frankness made me doubt the value of the exercise. The opportunity to chatter or gossip about themselves seemed to give them increased scope for self-indulgence and self-satisfaction.

All this time I had in my mind, as I remember it, an equally high ideal of what the truly helpful person should be like. Although I had never really confided in anyone older than myself, I suppose it was based on the sort of person I imagined I should value if I was in trouble. In my adolescence there were rather few adults I really admired, and most of these were not in the mould of this model helper at all. They were individuals who, in their own special spheres, seemed charismatically brilliant, skilful, articulate or beautiful. Some of those with whom I was more closely involved, who more often *tried* to be helpful, seemed by contrast dull, phoney and hypocritical. Their clumsy efforts to make useful comments or give interested attention seemed irrelevant and more calculated to emphasise their own value and experience, thus giving helping a bad name.

My model helpers were exceptional in a different way. One or two schoolmasters were specially expressive or sensitive in their teaching, which gave the impression of a kind of depth and power of feeling I knew I lacked. One or two clergymen seemed to have the sort of personal integrity, based on genuine humanity, self-knowledge and self-discipline, that I associated with the true helper. I imagined they had achieved these qualities through an intensity of feeling for others, which had allowed them a special kind of intuition or insight. Perhaps this could be learnt or acquired. I felt that this sort of person was more complete and whole than any other kind of adult I had met, and sometimes wanted to become more like them. Yet at other times the notion of myself as this kind of helper seemed absurd. I was not really someone in whom others confided – I must have seemed far too young, inexperienced and innocent. The things I enjoyed doing were emotionally undemanding and shallow. I was not very 'good with people', specially in large groups.

It can be seen that, at the stage when I was choosing a career, my notions of helping and the helper contained a good deal of muddle, idealisation and naiveté. But there was another element that precipitated my choice of a job when I left University – my identification with the underdog. I had always believed in – even before I was brave enough to insist upon – every person's right to be treated as worthy of respect, despite whatever made him odd, awkward or unattractive. This was probably because from childhood the inside of me had felt an outsider and an inadequate failure, even when the outside performed wonders of athleticism or scholarship. The inside felt at one with the public outcast and the grotesque buffoon. Furthermore, the social position of the deprived and deviant seemed so much more honourable than that of the privileged, and in some ways more fun.

The guilt I felt about my educational privileges was greatly reinforced when a close schoolfriend went to prison during my university years. This must have influenced my decision to work in a borstal. It was a very odd decision. Only someone whose motivation was pretty unrealistic and confused could have imagined that his concern for the disadvantaged would find a very positive expression in the role of a borstal officer. I was far too young and insecure to be able to handle the unpleasantly authoritarian aspects of the job and have enough energy or initiative left over to be helpful. My good intentions were of little use as I struggled to cope with hostility and my own ambivalence about the regulations. Only on the sports field, where I was sufficiently confident to relax, did I experience the kind of natural fellow-feeling that led spontaneously to liking and sharing. At such times I felt deeply grateful to the borstal boys who, in gestures or facial expressions more often than in words, acknowledged me as a fellow human being in spite of my status, and admitted me, however temporarily and provisionally, to the fraternity by which they endured their sentences.

After about a year, I fled from my discomfort and incompetence in the borstal and joined the probation service. I have rediscovered in an old file the rather clumsily expressed rationalisations by which I justified this change, in my application for social work training. 'I feel temperamentally attracted towards a job in which the people with whom I shall be dealing are in their normal, rather than in a confined and strictly disciplined, environment. I also feel that my years at a grammar school and later at a university should help me to be able to deal with a wider variety of people than the rather specialised section to be met at a borstal.'

Surprisingly enough, despite the confusion and naiveté I have described, some aspects of helping in social work seemed to come fairly naturally to me. I was not tempted to pity people or give them sympathy. I quickly recognised that true help involved getting alongside my clients, feeling with them rather than for them. I did not feel impelled to offer them false reassurance or to disarm them. I was not over-anxious to present myself as nice and helpful. I was aware of people's right to make their own choices and their own mistakes.

I owed many of these better instincts to my early family life. My family had been large, energetic, argumentative and quick to rise to any challenge. We were conscious of our distinguishing interests and personalities. We knocked sparks off each other. We often expressed solidarity and affection through mockery, and we enjoyed the cut and thrust of verbal battles. We were loyal to and proud of each other, but we seldom reassured or cossetted one another. We took ourselves seriously, but poured scorn on solemnity and poked fun at affectation or pomposity. All this made me rather resilient in situations of conflict. I found I had the capacity to survive it without disarming the protagonists, and to see love and need beneath abuse and recrimination. When I met hostile, mistrustful people I did not become specially tense, or need to insist that I was likeable and helpful.

But the same experiences had left me with an Achilles heel. My own great fear was loneliness, the feeling of being lost and abandoned. I needed little comfort but much company. Something about the rejection of vulnerable people, separating them from familiar sources of security, brought a tightness to my throat and tears to my eyes. When I could see the hurt and helpless infant in adults, I could hardly bear it. People driven by fear of separation and loss gripped me in their terror, and I would offer myself as a hostage to their despair. Only years of hard lessons, and mistakes through which my clients suffered, have taught me that the fear of being alone, like every other fear, can only be conquered when it is faced and survived.

Along with this weakness, I often underestimated the destructiveness and distortion of close relationships. From an early stage in my work, I began to appreciate the damage done in families by processes of communication too deep and powerful to be recognised by the ordinary senses. I linked this in my own mind with the strength and irrationality of early attachments, and with the desperate neediness of the young child. I could see that later attachments could be based on equally compulsive and unsound investments in others. Yet somehow these perceptions co-existed with an optimism about the benefits of family relationships, and the positive value of their survival, which was quite incompatible with them. I could not yet encompass the notion that some people did not begin to live until they had endured the pain of breaking a destructive relationship. Or rather I paid lip-service to such a notion, while my actions as a social worker belied it.

Linked with this was my difficulty in using constructively certain of the painful feelings aroused in me by my client's predicaments. I recognised that both the people themselves and their circumstances called forth reactions from a primitive level of my experience, and that it was important to handle these in a way which combined empathy and realism. In some situations I seemed able to achieve this. For instance, if a man cried when I visited him in prison I was able to allow and encourage him to express his grief and shame, to stay with it, even though it made me feel terrible. I did not interrupt him, mop him up or exhort him to think of the future. But there were other situations which I found much harder, because the feelings they provoked in me were more difficult to reconcile with my notion of what a helper should be like.

I can now see that I had largely retained my original ideal of the model helper, based as it was on adults I had perceived as possessing an extraordinary degree of integrity, humility and selflessness when I had been an adolescent. This ideal had only been partly modified by my social work training. My tutors, fieldwork supervisors and colleagues were more human models who could be more readily emulated, identified with and borrowed from. Yet beneath those recent experiences, and stronger than them, was the notion of a helper with superhuman powers of self-discipline and sensitivity. I could only be such a helper if my own unworthy needs and desires were somehow driven out by a pure and altruistic concern for others.

It was this, above all else, that made me so unrealistic in my long-term work with some very deprived people (an example of which will be given in chapter 4). The role of a counsellor to the weeping man in prison was consistent with the ideal helper; the role of a probation officer who refused to turn out in the evening to yet another crisis in the chaotic Barton family was not. In the process of trying to turn myself (largely unconsciously) into this totally reliable and dedicated social worker, I not only did violence to much of my own real nature. I was also profoundly unhelpful, because my reactions were based on a fantasy, on my ideal of myself, and not on the reality of the clients' circumstances. In ceasing to be true to many of my own feelings, or to reflect them in my behaviour towards these clients, I had also lost touch with much of what they were trying to communicate to me.

I now no longer imagine that being a good social worker involves moving onto a higher plane of ethical or emotional being. It does not mean becoming or being especially good. It requires a kind of self-knowledge and self-discipline, but not the kind I first imagined. It means knowing more about those parts of oneself which one might otherwise want to keep hidden from oneself, and learning to use them constructively, for others' benefit. It requires that one recognises, through one's reactions to clients, that one has within oneself all the same potentialities for destructiveness, despair, cruelty and crime that are manifested in their behaviour. It means having stirred up in one all these bad feelings, accepting that they are truly parts of oneself, yet learning to feel safe with them, to share them with clients. This is different from the kind of ascetic self-denial which was my original ideal. Instead of driving out the nasty parts of myself through dedication to my clients' interests, I have had to learn to accept these things in myself as a step towards giving true help to others. I have also had to learn to live with frustration, uncertainty and failure.

Nowadays, being a social worker does not feel at all like being a better person in the sense of my first notion. In many ways, it often feels more like living in a very difficult personal relationship. It involves being in a perpetual state of doubt, and above all, doubt whether it is all worth while. It involves alternating between the rather subtle pleasures of getting it more or less right (or so it seems at the time), and the despair of getting it all wrong. It means depending completely on the other person, and his perception of what is happening, its value and its meaning. It requires constant readjustments of perceptions, never allowing anything to be settled or final. It involves horrid feelings of meaninglessness and drift, of the pointlessness of all effort, of total abandonment, the fruitlessness of the past and the hopelessness of the future. The lack of personal connection at times produces an agonising mixture of guilt and resentment, an angry stuckness. Disengagement is impossible, yet so is progress. It sometimes feels like a nightmare stalemate.

Yet there are other times which are uplifting and invigorating. There are moments when I find the strength to make a stand, or take a risk, or break a pattern, and when the other person responds in kind. Or when each suddenly recognises a reaching out from the other, or an unexpected turning point, or the end of an old battle. There are wry and reluctant concessions, grudging acknowledgments, even some gruff gratitudes on both sides. At such moments, having survived the stalemate seems well worth the persistence and effort required.

All this is very different from my first notions of helping. By what processes have these fairly fundamental changes in my attitudes occurred? Largely, my views have altered through lessons which, directly or indirectly, my clients taught me. From the start, I recognised that social work, even with the best of intentions, could as readily be unhelpful as helpful. It was clear to me that every attempt to influence a person in trouble entailed a risk of making things worse for him, and that social work often did just this. Far more painful for me was the gradual recognition that often it was when I minded most about my clients, tried hardest or liked them best that I did them most harm. The risks of damage were highest where the investment was greatest.

One day during my first year as a probation officer, two young men walked into the office and said they were both on borstal licence, and had been travelling the country together. They were an unlikely pair. One of them, David James, was evidently articulate and intelligent in a pleasant, shy way. The other, Ron Grott, was dim and evasive. For some reason (I think we wanted to split them up) my colleague suggested that we should each supervise one of them, so we tossed a coin to see who would interview whom. To my relief, I won David, and I soon began to enjoy my meetings with him, while my colleague groaned at the thought of Ron's visits to the office. But within a few weeks, David was in trouble again for a serious offence, and given a long sentence of imprisonment, whereas Ron completed his licence satisfactorily and settled down. In my visits to David in prison, we identified a pattern of how repeatedly he had made 'good relationships' with probation officers, who 'helped' him separate from unsuitable friends, only for him to reoffend straight afterwards. In some mysterious way I had actually precipitated his reconviction. David and I planned that he should never, on leaving prison, go to see a probation officer again. Years later I sat in another prison making a similar plan with another immensely likeable young man with whom I had spent many hours over several years, but who somehow, in spite of his often expressed devotion and gratitude to me, always 'let me down'. I have some evidence that both these plans were subsequently followed to very good effect.

As well as recognising that I could, in some cases, be unintentionally but consistently unhelpful, I have also learnt from specific mistakes. I could not escape the links between things I had said or done at certain times and various bad consequences for my clients. I found that by looking these mistakes directly in the eye, by seeing them as they were and acknowledging them as my own, I could change, and do better. First I had fully to accept what I had done (neither exaggerating nor diminishing my part in the disaster), and then to look for ways of improving. I found that it was not shameful to admit to others that I had made a mistake; indeed it was essential to do so as part of the process of changing. What was more, admitting this to clients and examining how it had happened was often an important step in the sharing that led to true helping.

What at first I found hardest to acknowledge was where I had departed from my ideals and principles in my responses to clients. I might make mistakes, but I clung to the notion that certain cherished beliefs and attitudes must be inviolable. I was shocked to find that I sometimes seemed to offend these principles, and I tried to hide this from myself. But gradually I have come to recognise how these 'deviations' and 'lapses' are usually the keys to growth and development in helping. The feelings and experiences on which they are based are more real than the ideals they challenge. If I can accept the parts of myself they signal, then I can begin to use these more constructively and creatively in my work. Instead of trying to deny and split off these aspects of myself, I can integrate them with the others that I have found more acceptable. It now seems to me to be a first principle of social work that I should be open to all my reactions to clients, and ready to adapt and modify all my other principles. Otherwise they are in danger of becoming rigid and deadening rules of thumb.

What therefore remains of my original ideals? All of them have been modified, at least in relation to their use in helping as a social worker. For instance, I have been forced to re-examine my concern for the underdog. My identification and championship were from a position of strength and achievement. However much of an underdog I might have felt, my performance belied these feelings, so I often appeared to be fighting battles that were not my own. I have only slowly learnt how much harder it is to be brave and committed to the unfortunate from a position of weakness and vulnerability. It has taken me even longer to learn to share with others the things about myself which I regarded as most inadequate and blameworthy. Yet I now feel, through having allowed others to know about my failures, more secure, honest and realistic in my relationships with clients who feel ashamed and despised.

Of these original ideals, the one which has best stood the test of time and experience has been the value of communication between the middles of people. My first notion of this was rather mystical and magical, that it stemmed from someone's special intuitive powers. It was as if such a gifted person could suddenly penetrate an otherwise private inner core of another's mind by a flash of inspired insight. This demanded extraordinary perceptive and communicative skills. Now I see this sort of truth-to-truth feeling as attainable for all of us in our daily transactions with each other. Often when it happens it is not because of a specially insightful comment, but because the deeper significance of an everyday encounter between people is tacitly recognised and shared. This may more readily occur amongst very simple, ordinary or inarticulate people than between educated or gifted ones. For instance, a group of children may suddenly notice one of their number doing something, all on his own, that he has never been able to do before, and respond with a spontaneous round of applause.

In many situations – in teaching as well as social work – words and actions which cut through incidentals to reach essentials seem to release energy and vitality and leave people freer to tackle important issues. 'Getting to the heart of the matter' seems to suggest simultaneously reaching an emotional as well as a logical truth. It releases creative and constructive imagination and dynamism. The opposite feeling, of being unable to reach the middle of someone who is important to us, is frustrating and dispiriting.

The helper's own supplies of energy and enthusiasm seem to me to be closely related to his ability to establish communication with the middles of his clients. The creative and invigorating aspects of social work lie in making contact with someone who has previously shut off. To remain genuinely responsive, he depends on opportunities to see through the incidentals to the real issues and the real person. I no longer think of this in terms of specially deep or penetrative insights, but more in terms of staying tuned-in to the clients with all my faculties, and trusting apparently random hunches or strange associations. I look for signs (often just fleeting facial expressions) of humour and strength in the seemingly depressed and hopeless, or of vulnerability in the apparently confident, and try to reach these hidden parts of a person as soon as I recognise them. Often real helping stems from a seemingly chance remark that suddenly becomes meaningful, and leads to a new way of looking at some problem that has been oppressive and imprisoning. This experience can feel as liberating to the social worker as to the client.

2
Being helped

I want to turn now from the origins of the helper's attitudes and motives to the process of helping. Most of us are most familiar with this process through being helped. We have had others in whom we chose to confide our troubles; or helpful colleagues on whose advice and assistance we relied; or mentors who taught us important lessons in life; or superiors whom we respect. We have had others still who did us good simply by their presence, or who made us feel better just to see them.

There are obvious differences between these kinds of help, and if we are fortunate we may have a wide circle of people from whom we can get each kind as we need it. There are undoubtedly counterparts to all these different varieties of help which can be made available to people in trouble. In later chapters I shall suggest that social work should encompass many other sorts of helping besides that provided by individual social workers. But it is hard to escape the conclusion that every social worker should be able to give a certain kind of help when it is needed, and that this corresponds to one sort of help which is much prized in friendships and other personal relationships. This is based on a tacit understanding that some situations require one person to recognise and respond to the needs of another, to suspend his own needs and concentrate on the other's. In most good friendships this understanding is a sort of reciprocal agreement, and is within a context of give and take, and of sharing many other experiences and activities. However, in the last resort we tend to judge our closest friends by their responses when we are really distressed about something, and at such moments we expect them to appreciate that we need help, and focus their attention on that need, at the expense of their own preoccupations.

The first and most important aspect of this helpful attention is the quality of listening. I would suggest that good listening is an art. It is something active and creative, not something passive. There is a qualitative difference between being listened to with real concern and compassion, and being listened to simply in the sense of being received loud and clear. Listening is not just hearing, and is not just done with the ears. The feelings of the listener – communicated usually most effectively in non-verbal ways – are all-important to the quality of active, creative listening. The good listener encompasses the other person's experiences and feelings within his own experiences and feelings. Even if he has never been in the same situation, or had the same emotions, there is a reaching out to the other person, an attempt to relate the other person's reality to his own.

When I have felt that someone has been listening helpfully to what I am saying, I have felt that he was listening with the whole of himself, not just a part. It is as if he wants to experience what I am saying and feeling in himself. Although I cannot say quite how I know it, or what clues he gives me, I do somehow know that my feelings are echoing and reverberating inside him with his feelings, that he is emotionally tuned in to what I am saying. The quality of his listening conveys itself to me in ways other than the words he speaks. (There may be many different non-verbal clues which suggest that someone is listening well. I suspect that they consist of minute changes of expression or posture which indicate that the significance of something described has been registered. These changes indicate the evocation of a response which is probably more important than words to someone who is uneasy or distressed.)

These qualities of good listening can be contrasted with the sort of responses we are all familiar with from our less successful attempts to talk to others. Someone who is not a good listener makes invisible barriers between himself and myself. He treats me as an alien, outside, other than himself, different in kind. He makes me feel conscious of what I am saying as increasing the gulf between us. Again, this is conveyed non-verbally, and is a quality of the relation between his feelings and mine. Very often his words bear no direct relation to the way I feel his emotional reaction to me. He may well be saying, 'Yes, yes, quite, quite . . . ,' or even 'I understand', or 'I know how it feels'. Yet I sense that he does not encompass me or my situation in his own experience, he does not listen to me with the whole of himself. He simply switches on a 'listening to people's problems' part of himself, with accompanying noises. Somehow, his words have the opposite effect to that intended – they convince me that he does not understand. His real feelings, of detachment or even hostility, come through to me more strongly than the message his words are intended to convey.

Good listening is the beginning of any helping process, and an important part of its continuation. It is the basis of the helpful response, because by ensuring that the helper is tuned in to all the wavelengths of the troubled person's message, it makes it possible for the helper to respond to the whole of what is being told him. This is important, because the very essence of feeling troubled, distressed, uneasy or helpless is usually ambivalence. Strong feelings are sometimes overwhelmingly forceful and primitive, and we may do something very impulsive and wrong while we are in the grip of them; but it is usually *mixed* feelings that cause us to seek help. It is the conflict of emotions which leaves us so uncertain and ill at ease. Thus the helper has to be able to hear more than one message at once, and has to be able to be alive to contradictions and inconsistencies in what he is told. If he is listening with the whole of himself, with his feelings as well as his mind, he himself will experience some of the discomfort of my ambivalence.

The word 'empathy' is often used about the helping process. It implies that the helper 'feels with' the person in trouble; that by imaginatively entering the other's situation, he engages his own emotions in such a way as to share the other's responses. I am suggesting that this is an essential part of helping. But it is also a risky business. If the helper is not tuned in to all the aspects of the other person's conflicting feelings, his empathy will be one-sided, partial, incomplete and ultimately unhelpful. Partial empathy seems to me to be what old-style social work theorists were describing when they wrote about 'over-involvement' and 'over-identification'. What I think they meant was that the helper picked up part of the other person's feelings, and responded strongly to these, perhaps additionally reinforcing them with reactions of his own. This produced a reaction which was false and unhelpful, because it missed the equally important other side of the coin, the feeling which was in conflict with the one picked up.

We can recognise this in our experiences of seeking help. We often choose to confide in someone who will be 'understanding', in the sense that he will accept our characteristic weaknesses or failings, will recognise some validity in our unorthodoxies and some virtue in our vices. It is easier to confess to someone who is likley to follow the steps that have led us into whatever moral swamp we have entered, to see our reasons for starting and continuing down that path. But we have also often had the experience of feeling first rather frustrated and then guilty, annoyed or betrayed, when that acceptance prevents our confidant from hearing the other part of our story. We often do not simply want to be understood – to be told, in effect, that he too has been there, or could easily have got there but for a stroke of luck. We may even want to find a way back. We want him also to hear why our situation is bad or wrong or uncomfortable for us, or for others. We do not want him to excuse us, protect us or apologise for us. We want him to help us find the strength to resolve our own conflict, in our own way.

Partial empathy is often exhilarating and exciting for the helper, and gives short-term relief to the other person. There is a delight and joy in the recognition and the sharing which comes from total identification with another, but it tends to be short-lived. The true empathy which stems from sharing the pain and confusion of another person's emotional and moral conflicts is usually less dramatic, but in the long run almost always more effective. It demands much more self-discipline. It is not the rather defensive 'controlled involvement' of the old-style theorists, but rather the whole, as opposed to the partial, involvement of the helper. It requires the exercise of all his intuitive and imaginative capacities rather than simply an easy response to one of the themes of the other's message.

The true helper, in my experience, allows me to develop my account of what is troubling me without cutting across it. He does not interrupt with redundant, irrelevant comments or reassurances. He lets me do my own work, rather than trying to do it for me. He lets me struggle to express things in my own way, lets me point out where I've gone wrong, correct myself when I've misled him. He doesn't take anything away from me. It is a natural reaction, when troubled by strong or conflicting feelings, to try to offload them onto someone else. Once again, it seems like a relief in the short run if we succeed in getting someone to do this. It feels as if we have been helpfully relieved of a burden if the helper 'takes on board' all my anger, or depression, or anxiety. Yet the true helper does not do this, because the help of sharing lies in learning to live with one's own feelings, not having them taken away. The true helper enables me to see that my feelings are manageable and bearable, by withstanding them with me, not taking them from me.

A great deal of the art of helping lies in letting the other person tell the helper the worst. Obviously, the whole point about the worst in any situation is that it is what we do not want to face. It is worst precisely because we cannot face it. If it was easy to face it, we would not need help. Because it is what is worst for us, we will not find it easy to say. The art of helping by sharing lies in knowing when the other person has not yet reached the worst, and letting him get there. This is largely a matter of self-knowledge and self-discipline. The helper feels very tempted to block the other person off from reaching the worst, because it is painful enough to share everything else that leads up to it. Very often it is the helper who cannot bear to hear the worst, rather than the other person who cannot bear to tell it. Again, I think we can all recall to mind times when we have tried to confide a dark secret, and our intended confidant has subtly refused to hear it.

There are many ways in which the helper can cut the other

person short before he reaches the worst. One of these is by insisting that he understands, that there is no need to say any more. Another is by elaborating and complicating a particular point so that he gets stuck at it. Another is to interject some clever interpretation or tricky question which confuses the other person by suggesting that he sees all sorts of deeper implications in what has been said. Another is simply to bring the conversation to an end. All these are ways of switching off from listening and sharing beyond a certain point, and all are essentially self-defensive for the helper. Partial empathy is often a manifestation of such a defence – the helper gets stuck in one aspect of the other's feelings because he cannot bear to hear the others.

However, there are of course always times when we are so confused, upset or ashamed about ourselves and our situations that we fail to tell the whole story. The extent to which our failures are conscious failures must vary considerably. I suspect we are all dimly aware of bad faith when we distort our feelings or convey them only partially. We are at least partly conscious of our emotional dishonesties. We know that it is courage we mostly lack, and not insight – the courage to look at ourselves and the realities of our circumstances, rather than to deceive and reassure ourselves. The mere presence of some helpers, their sheer integrity, or straightforwardness or goodwill, often in itself gives us more courage than we would usually possess. It is very difficult to be shallow or pusillanimous with some helpers, because they set such high standards of honesty themselves. Yet there will always be some times when we need the help of a comment, or the jolt of contradiction, to get nearer the truth. There is an art of helping which consists of saying something that moves the other person onwards towards telling and facing the worst, as a step towards resolving his conflict.

In the theoretical literature of social work, this art has often been confused with the techniques of psychotherapy. A great deal has been written about when it is appropriate to 'offer insight' or 'make interpretations'. Most of this seems to miss the point. Many of our feelings and motives are probably beyond the reach of our consciousness for much of the time, but this is seldom relevant to the help we seek with our immediate problems. Those of us who seek help with problems arising from our day-to-day lives are seldom in search of therapy, and seldom need it. This is fortunate, as little is available, and it is a costly business. Most helpers have to assume that the other person has within him the resources to resolve his conflicts, and most of us who seek help share this assumption. It is reasonable to suppose that we can find the courage to face ourselves and our situations as they are, rather than needing to retreat from them into the asylum and artificiality of the therapeutic milieu. On this assumption the helper's task is not to explore what is out of reach of consciousness (a task which requires the safety of the therapeutic environment) but simply to develop the trust which is necessary before very painful truths can be shared.

Every helper has to face the fact that other people do not particularly want to experience pain and shame. He also has to face his own resistance to sharing such bad feelings. Hence there are strong reasons why both he and the other person may avoid or resist getting to the worst. Where the other person shows signs he is doing this, becoming distracted, evasive, repeating himself, responding inappropriately, being over-insistent or false in some other way, he has to decide whether to try to help him move on, and how to do so. The first decision usually involves understanding and measuring his own feelings. He will probably sense a great resistance (often in the form of fear) in himself, which tells him to let the other person get away with his defensive tactics. It is usually possible to rationalise this fear, to give it some objective status. The other person has had enough, is too tired, upset or frail to go on. There is nothing to be gained by doing so. It can all wait till another time. Obviously there is often good sense in these thoughts, and it is often right to act on them. But the helper has to balance these gains against the possibility of losing a real opportunity of reaching a healing truth, and also the risk of the other person being disillusioned by his collusion with defensive tactics. As people in trouble, we have probably at times lost respect for helpers who have allowed themselves to be fobbed off by us, particularly if we suspected that they were really being self-protective in doing so.

The role of the helper assumes that it is difficult for the other person to do the right thing, to take a brave decision, to resolve a painful conflict. His role must therefore consist in part at least, of holding the other person to a difficult task. He must expect the other person to dodge and weave, to double back, to lose his way. He may need to be quietly but firmly insistent on holding him to the pain which is in him and in his situation. He will certainly have to cultivate the self-discipline to avoid collusion with escapes and deceptions if he wants to be really helpful; otherwise he will follow many wrong paths, be sent on many wild goose chases.

In my experience, the kind of person who helps me be truthful, who helps me get to the point of looking at the conflicts which are disabling me, is someone who is real and credible as a person himself. His responses are real, from the whole of himself. Even if he is wrong, or misunderstands me, he rings true, because he is saying what is real for him – and I am free to disagree with him. But on the whole such a person will recognise what is real and true in what I say, and also what is false, and he will not be afraid to say so in his own way. If I am irrelevant or inappropriate in what I say, he will sense it, and bring me back to the point. If I start to express feelings which are out of proportion and unnecessary, he will shut me up. He may get angry with me, and he won't mind me getting angry with him. But if he comments on what I have told him, it will not be just for the sake of being clever, or giving my 'problems' some new objective quality. He won't turn my difficulties into things, give them labels, wrap them up neatly in his ideas. He will share my real feelings with me, he will have feelings of his own, he will tell me when he thinks mine are distorted, and when he thinks I'm not being straight. Sometimes he will help me develop what I am thinking and feeling, or relate it to something else, usually something broader. Very often through him I will see that there are much deeper implications in the things that were bothering me than I realised before. But this will not be through his smart interpretations, but through the real wisdom that allows me to follow my own processes of thought. Somehow, without knowing why, I shall feel better after I've talked to him because I shall not have escaped from anything, or twisted anything. I shan't have been reassured or cossetted or treated like a child, but I shall have been recognised, treated as real, by a fellow human being.

In suggesting that to be effective the helper must be a real person, I am making it clear that I think helping is not simply a skill or expertise or technique. Helping is a test of the helper as a person. It involves the disciplined use of the whole of the personality. This includes the helper's own 'bad' feelings – his sadness, anger, fear, greed and cowardice. He has to be in touch with these things in himself in order to be truly open to the other person's distress. Yet he has also to retain his own values and standards, his own strengths and virtues. He has to recognise that the other person's feelings and fantasies are real to him, and to share in the discomfort of them, yet also to stay in touch with his own reality. Here again, as people in trouble we know the qualitative difference between a helper who is swept away by the force of our subjectivity, and one who, though deeply affected by it, still remains true to himself. Once more, it is a difference in the emotional quality of the relationship rather than in the words used. It is a difference that we feel.

By contrast, we can also feel when a would-be helper's offer of help is not real, and is not made with the whole of himself. We can sense when he is closed to our reality, to what is affecting us most deeply. We can tell when he is simply applying his moral rules of thumb to our situation, when he is cocksure of his own rightness, or when he is secretly saying to himself, 'Thank goodness I could never be so weak and foolish'. Perhaps even more annoyingly, we can sense when someone is seeming to offer us something very grand and total, which is essentially false. It promises involvement and commitment, but actually is detached, defensive and evasive. It seems sincere, but really it is mechanical and automatic. In a real crisis, challenged by strong feelings or important decisions, we know it will wilt and fade. Its comments are bland and trite, essentially smokescreens which conceal its true nature. This kind of 'helper' hasn't the honesty to admit that he has no time for us; that he is just waiting to get on with his real business, to pay his mortgage or to take his family out shopping. He has every right to have other priorities – but we too have a right to be told this. We might even have some respect for this, if only he would tell us straight. We feel justified in our anger because of his hypocrisy, his determination to appear helpful without incurring any cost to himself. Why doesn't he just admit to us and to himself that he doesn't care about us and our problems?

This has been a very brief and incomplete sketch of some of the processes of helping which take place between individuals in everyday life. Obviously, most of the help we receive does not take this form at all. We are equally glad and grateful of help which is much more practical and material in its content; of friends who are always cheerful; of others who are specially talented and skilful in different spheres; of others still whose style and sophistication draws us or whose simplicity and wholesomeness refreshes us. Even if we think of moments when we are tired, confused or in conflict with ourselves, we often get very different kinds of help from the ones I have described. At such moments, I usually find that my very old car, with which I wholly identify, breaks down. I then go to my mechanic, who works for himself, in a small dark oily shed. He nearly always mends the car at once, and usually in my presence. We talk sporadically while he is doing this, and I always feel much better. Without knowing it, he has helped me with much more than my broken car.

I want to turn now from helping in private relationships to the kind of help given by social workers. What I have described so far is the helpfulness of trusted friends and respected colleagues. To what extent can professional helpers aim at similar processes of helping? Do people who consult social workers even want this kind of help? Is it not presumptuous to claim to be a professional friend to people in distress?

The growth of state welfare organisations, and especially of local authority social services departments, has led social work to be associated with a number of relatively impersonal processes. In the public mind, 'The Welfare' is where you go to complain about the way your neighbour is treating her child; or that the old lady across the road is creating a fire risk; or to get a home help for your disabled uncle. It may also be where you go in desperation when you can't pay your electricity bill, or when you are about to be homeless, or when you can't get any sense out of some other local government department. Its powers and functions are vague and wide, and are associated with unpleasant things like child abuse, madness, death, poverty, juvenile delinquency and other reasons for being 'put away'. It is a place which is official, keeps records, investigates complaints. It is surrounded by an atmosphere of fear and mistrust, by stereotypes on the one hand of menacing authority, on the other of mystery and muddle. It has money, goods and services to give away, but it is far from clear to whom it gives them, or how much, or why.

At the end of this book, the developments in social policy which have contributed to these confused perceptions of social services departments will be further discussed. At this stage, the point I want to make is that it is by no means obvious to the public what sort of help is available from such departments, or indeed whether help with personal problems is likely to be given in a personal way. The very size and complexity of the organisations, the buildings, the waiting rooms and reception facilities, all give some pause for doubt on these points. They also sometimes influence social workers to question whether they are in business to provide personal help, or to make arrangements for a number of things to be done, given, moved, withdrawn or withheld, according to certain departmental criteria. Instructions and procedures, forms and regulations, sometimes appear to determine their dealings with clients to such an extent as to preclude all human contact.

Yet I am suggesting that in many situations what is required of the social worker is a kind of help which is seldom elsewhere available except from a certain kind of good friend. Of course, many clients will have no such expectation; and others will reject the offer of it. But to make no offer, to shrug off the expectation when it is present, to refuse to take responsibility for the personal and moral issues which clients may want to raise, all these attitudes seem both disrespectful to clients and unworthy of the social worker as a helper. It seems to me much safer to aim at these standards, and to find – usually to our relief – that they are not always required, than to assume that the faceless official or the expert therapist is all that the client can reasonably anticipate or practicably need. In so far as all of us expect and require more of others at times, a profession of helpers should have more than this to offer.

I have suggested that helping in social work should be directly based upon the lessons of helping in ordinary life. However, it would be wrong to pretend that there are not special problems about the role of a professional helper. In this chapter I want to look first at some general problems of professional helping, and then at some specific problems arising from the settings in which social work is practised.

One basic problem of professional helping lies in the fact that most social workers do it as a full-time job. They are expected to be available to people in trouble for at least forty hours a week, and usually more. Often, their offices are bombarded with new applications for help every day, and they have no effective control over the volume of their work. Their senses become dulled and their sensibilities blunted; they suffer from emotional saturation or drought. Their helping can become automatic, unspontaneous and quite joyless – they can come to resent their clients.

It would be quite unrealistic to deny that this happens. However, I want now to argue that the psychological state of exhaustion, apathy and resentment is not always a consequence of overwork or the pressure of new referrals, or even of departmental futility, dishonesty or callousness. It can be, and often is, a consequence of a fundamentally mistaken and misleading view of the process of professional helping. To this extent, social workers can become their own worst enemies, and in hindering themselves, can do harm to their clients.

I want to suggest that this psychological state results from a sterotype of helping which many social workers carry into their practice. It is as if the motivation to help others is based on a certain naive impulse which is split off from other aspects of experience. Obviously, the desire to help is a necessary part of every social worker's motives; but it is as if this impulse is not directly related to the kinds of experiences of being helped that I have described in this chapter. Nor is it related to other obviously relevant ideas or feelings – for instance, the insights into human nature available from novels, poems and plays. As a professional helper, the social worker neither sees his clients as human beings like himself nor sees them as like the people he imagines or identifies with or has read about in literature. His understanding of the human condition may be profound, but his helping remains at a very superficial, almost childlike level. Thus he is easily disillusioned, and can soon become cynical and apathetic.

I first began to notice and consider this phenomenon when teaching social work to groups of students. It became apparent from the use of role play as a teaching method. In order to study the person-to-person processes of social work, I asked one student to 'become' a client he found specially difficult to help, and another to take the part of the social worker. The method seemed rather artificial, and appeared to require acting skills to be effective. Yet almost without exception the students played their clients brilliantly. They conveyed all the subtleties and nuances of difficult people, presenting their problems in demanding or misleading ways. They portrayed the covert threats, the dark hints, the emotional blackmails, the ambivalences and ambiguities. The difficulties they gave those who tried to help them were 'real', in the sense that they tended to make the other student feel every bit as uncomfortable and ill-at-ease as they themselves had felt with their clients. A great deal of the problem of helping such people lay in the fact that they threw the social worker off balance by the urgency, the vehemence or the complexity of the manner in which they presented their needs. Yet there was also something more than this. The student social worker was hampered not only by the way the client behaved, but also by an apparent expectation of how he should behave. He seemed to feel that he should be nice, kind, tolerant and understanding, but the way this came across was essentially false. The falseness seemed to be something in the social work role itself, rather than in the artificiality of the role play. After all, the 'client' was real enough – he seemed very free to improvise, to be spontaneously wicked, mixed up, violent, threatening or seductive. Naturalness and originality were no problem to him. Yet the social worker seemed always to be in a kind of self-imposed straitjacket, consisting of his own rather narrow stereotype of his role.

Having once become aware of this phenomenon, I began to notice it in other situations – in reading the records of interviews kept by social workers, in observing them at work, and so on. There seemed to be a state of mind (often reflected in a physical posture) associated with the stereotypical professional helper. The social worker was rather stilted, inhibited, unexpressive and limited in every way. He was heavy, yet without any real authority. He was anxious without being sensitive. He was evasive rather than subtle. He was more defensive than careful. He was earnest without being sincere. But above all, he wanted to help, and to be seen as helpful. He listened without really listening, and hurried on towards the 'helpful' solution to the client's problem, before the client had time to define it. His answers were much too easy, and they met his needs, not the client's. He seemed more concerned to play his 'helping' role, within the limits of its defining mannerisms, than truly to help the client.

In the case of the students in the role plays, this phenomenon was striking, because they gave evidence that their stilted performance as social workers was not based on a failure to understand or get inside the client. They knew him, his moods, his conflicts and contradictions, well enough to portray him very accurately when they took his part. It was not that their imaginative range could not encompass his emotions or enter his situation. It was not that they could not get in touch with the depressed or the delinquent or the mad parts of themselves. It was rather that *as social workers* they could not get in touch with them. Something about the role of social worker fixed them, locked them, imprisoned them in a set of stereotyped responses from which they could not depart.

In the first chapter, I tried to give some account of the development of my own concept of helping, and the attitudes and motives that led me to become a social worker. I tried to indicate some of the ways in which I now see my original motivation as suspect, based as it was on my early stereotypes of the helpful adult, and my childhood experiences of love and loss in my immediate relationships. What I want to suggest now is that all social workers carry some such stereotypes and childish feelings into their professional practice, and that they can become locked in a state of mind about helping their clients which is derived from these original attitudes and emotions. When this occurs, they stop learning from experience, and above all, they do not learn from their mistakes and failures to help. Instead, much of their emotional energy is directed towards protecting their original notion of helping from the assaults of such experiences.

I shall refer to this original motivation and its accompanying attitudes by the shorthand title 'naive helpfulness'. As I hope I have illustrated from my own case, this does not imply that it is simple, or based on a single thread of feeling or faith. It can be, and in my case was, the product of a fairly complex interaction of early and later relationships. But it is likely to incorporate aspects of the self and of others in which difficult episodes and emotions have not been fully resolved. For instance, my own motivation contained a strong but unrecognised desire to protect vulnerable people from the pain of separation and rejection. This naive impulse was so strong that I tended to split it off from my other ideas and 'principles', and to shield it from the consequences of my actions. I was not prepared to learn that I was not helping those clients whom I tried to place under this kind of protection.

As I have tried to illustrate in the first chapter, the desire to become a social worker contains many diverse and sometimes incompatible elements. Those which I call 'naive' are distinguished mainly by their inaccessibility. They are not easily elicited in discussion, nor are they closely related to other notions derived from experiences of helping and being helped. Often they are in direct conflict with ideas about the human condition derived from other sources – from reading, the theatre or the cinema. Thus, although the social worker may think deeply and be highly sensitive to a client's feelings, he is none the less locked into a certain way of responding. Time and again a pattern of words and actions is triggered off by the client's distress, which is satisfying for neither.

The form such naiveté takes is often an insistence by the social worker on hearing only part of what the client is telling him. The social worker almost wilfully ignores a great many indications, or even vehement assertions by the client, that the situation is different from, and usually worse than, the worker wants to understand it to be. The social worker's naiveté may consist in refusing to make connections between facts, or to appreciate conflicts of feelings, or to draw conclusions from circumstances, or to accept consequences of situations. He obstinately continues to give his form of 'help' in wilful disregard of some highly relevant and very obvious element which renders it ineffective. Then, when the crisis or disaster occurs, it is quite 'unexpected', and he draws the most negative conclusions about his client, whom he condemns for his failure to take advantage of all the assistance given him.

All professional helpers can be guilty of this sort of disingenuousness at times. I myself was disastrously at fault in this way soon after I started work in the mental hospital. A patient in her fifties insisted that she was suffering from the long-term consequences of venereal disease in her youth, that she was rotting away from the inside, was foul smelling and putrid. There was no medical or physical evidence either of the alleged cause of her condition or of the condition itself. Yet the obvious conclusion, that she was deeply depressed, was not borne out by her other behaviour or by her responses to treatment. She stayed in hospital for several months, and although she was for most of this time on no drugs, she got neither much better nor any worse. After the first few weeks, when she said she was unable to walk or keep her balance, her behaviour was quite normal – she ate and slept normally, walked in the grounds and communicated with other patients. Yet she insisted that she was dying, and should stay in hospital till she died. By this time she had been transferred to a ward away from where I worked, and I only saw her occasionally for a talk. One day she told me that her doctor and her new social worker had arranged for her to go to live in a registered home several miles from the hospital. She said she felt this was a wrong decision, as she would prefer to stay in hospital for the rest of her life. I found myself pointing out that she had no physical need to be in hospital, that she received no nursing care or physical attention, nor indeed any psychological treatment. I wondered why she could not accept that she still had a life of her own, which was hers. She could choose to do what she pleased with the rest of her life, however long it might be. Within a week of being discharged to the home, she committed suicide by hanging herself.

What horrified me most about my part in this was my total surprise when I heard this news. I had never thought of her as any sort of suicide risk. Yet she had been telling me consistently that she wanted to die, and had nothing to live for. I had refused to understand what she said. Even though I was no longer directly involved in decisions such as the one to discharge her, I should have been listening better to her, and I should have given her a better chance to talk about her worst fears. Even if her decision to kill herself was an example of a definite choice by her, of the kind I was suggesting, I had failed to recognise this as one of the choices open to her. When someone is very preoccupied with death, suicide is always a possibility. It was naive of me to fail to recognise this with her. I should at least have acknowledged this possibility to myself, and probably also to her. My failure to do so showed that I had not allowed myself to share her feelings, but preferred to cling to an unrealistic notion both of her, and of myself as a helper in relation to her.

I can remember a similar phenomenon from my early days as a probation officer. Occasionally, clients who ostensibly were trying to give me a very good impression of themselves and their circumstances would convey in some other way that all was far from well. By something they said or didn't say, some contradiction or other indication, they gave a clear signal that they were again committing offences, or about to do so. But I refused to take heed of this message, and acted as if I believed all the good things they were telling me about themselves. Then, when I was informed by the police that they had been arrested, I would feel first shock, and then discomfort and guilt. When I allowed myself to look at the latter feeling, I could recognise that I had really known all along. (In fact I proved this to myself later by asking my secretary never to tell me which of my clients was in trouble when she heard from the police, but to let me guess; I was nearly always right in one of my first two guesses.) My original need to deny that I knew, to pretend to the client that I believed his false version of himself, was very unhelpful, because it usually provoked the client into further offences or at least allowed him to go on commiting offences and to get himself deeper into trouble. The result was that in the end he faced far more serious charges than if he had managed to get me to face the worst with him earlier. I suspect that it was more my need to be the kindly probation officer, pleased with my client's achievements, than his need to deceive me that was responsible for this evasion. It is not easy to draw someone's attention to the indications that he is probably breaking the law again, or in danger of doing so. It requires that the probation officer cares enough about trying to keep his client out of prison to risk damaging his 'good relationship' by angering him greatly – perhaps even by drawing quite false inferences, and being wrong. But there are tactful and humble ways of taking this risk, just as there are ways of apologising when we are wrong; and clients can usually recognise when we make a mistake in good faith. Geoffrey Parkinson, in one of his *New Society* articles about probation, wrote that he used to tell clients he suspected of going off the rails that he had dreamt that they were in trouble again. This seems a rather nice way of conveying to the client that one has had a not entirely reliable intuition about him, but one which leaves him free to say, 'Well, it's funny you should say that Mr. Parkinson, but . . . '

There are aspects of the role of the professional social worker, especially in statutory agencies, which reinforce workers' tendencies towards naive helpfulness. The worker is part of a large organisation, and officially connected with even more powerful institutions such as the law, hospitals or social security. He is seen therefore as having the means to solve problems by decisive intervention. The client is often anxious to unburden himself of the pain and responsibility of his situation, and to pass these on to the social worker and his agency. If the worker's naive motivation includes a desire to relieve realistic anxiety or to solve unresolvable problems, then these expectations, however distorted and destructive, will be unbearable and irresistible for him. He will be willing to assume responsibility for and control of aspects of the client's predicament which hurt, but his decision to do so will be based more on his needs than the client's, and he will do so in a way which is fundamentally unhelpful.

As the powers and duties of social workers in social services departments have become wider and vaguer (in the public mind), it becomes more and more important that social workers convey to confused and desperate clients the limits of their helpfulness and the dangers of drastic outcomes from their interventions. Social services departments can give various forms of assistance, including material benefits and practical services. But they can also remove children, lock up delinquents, and admit others to various residential institutions. The careers of social work clients often begin with receiving the former assistance and end in one of the latter outcomes. Progress through the stages in between is seldom marked by warning signs or diversions. The social worker's 'helpfulness' can lead the client along this road, beckoning him with the smiles and reassurances of an indulgent parent.

In many ways, developments in social policy and in the administration and practice of social services departments have further contributed to the growth of this form of naive helpfulness. There is a trend towards a style of work which is paternalistic and protective towards clients. It has become quite ambiguous, whether material aid and other services are offered because people are specially needy, or because they are specially difficult, destructive or 'at risk'. It is ambiguous whether these things are to be seen as rights or privileges; whether social workers give them from motives of generosity or suspicion; whether they believe clients require help or whether they are using help as a pretext to watch over them. There is also ambiguity and confusion about social workers' statutory powers to remove vulnerable or deviant individuals, or to detain them compulsorily or arrange voluntary admissions to institutions. These powers are often not spelt out to clients, nor is it clear to what extent they are used as treatment, as protection, or as punishment in any circumstances. The social worker is sometimes encouraged by his agency's policies to pose as a helper, who is endlessly understanding and persevering, but who is reluctantly forced into using these heavy measures, for clients' own good, because they behave in irrational, unpredictable ways, and thus reject the help given them.

I would argue that this paternalistic trend in policy plays very directly into social workers' need to be naively helpful. The role of the social worker which these policies prescribe is very like that of long-suffering and pseudo-tolerant parents who are always being let down by their difficult children. I think a great deal of social workers' motivation to be naively helpful stems from an internalisation of their own parents' protectiveness towards them. As children we all tended to be baled out of situations by our parents, to be protected from the consequences of our initiatives and explorations. Sometimes we were overprotected, prevented from having any real feelings or real experiences. If this occurred, one part of us rebelled against it, but another absorbed it uncritically, as a model of loving, parental behaviour. Too often, I believe, this part of his experience is precisely the part which forms the social worker's 'sacred core' of motivation, his model of helpfulness. He simply reproduces with his clients what he had done as a small child to him. The paternalistic tendency of social policy seems to validate this approach to his work. It suggests that clients should be treated as children; that they should be indulged up to a point, because they are so impulsive and irresponsible, but then controlled, if necessary by taking decisions out of their hands. It suggests that like children they cannot be expected to understand themselves, the world, or the consequences of their actions, or necessarily to understand why their parents are acting, firmly and responsibly, in doing things for them – except that it is 'for their own good'.

I have argued that the only effective antidote to naive helpfulness is an honest and self-critical approach, based on good listening to the whole of what the client is telling, and a self-disciplined attempt to respond to his needs. Some problems which bring clients to social workers are such that this is very difficult. Material problems are a good example. They create a special kind of gap or barrier between client and worker. If a client is destitute this is simply a fact. It is also a fact that most social workers have some powers and some resources, however limited, to dispense money. This provokes feelings both of guilt and of sympathy in the social worker, and it focuses his attention on one aspect of the client's needs, often at the expense of all others. It can trigger off a kind of naiveté, that consists in supposing that a small amount of immediate financial assistance (which relieves some of his guilt) is much more helpful than it can realistically be. The social worker is then surprised and upset when the client's subsequent reactions show him to be angry, ungrateful or exploitative of the worker's 'generosity'. Usually, the client is reacting to the worker's uncaring failure to recognise the wider and longer-term implications of his circumstances, and against the bad faith involved in an inadequate, partial response, which the worker should, if he was honest, be able to see was no real help to the client.

Homelessness is perhaps even more difficult than destitution, because it focuses the social worker's attention on his personal life and circumstances. A homeless person always seems to be asking, 'Why can't I come and live in your house?' He makes the social worker conscious of his investments in property, including the property of his career and private obligations, and of how exclusive and self-protective his life-style is. He makes the worker aware of how he uses his privacy as a defence, and as a limit on his offer of help. The worker's guilty consciousness of the severe restrictions he places on what he is willing to do to help can make him try even harder, and more falsely, to be 'helpful'. Instead of being honest about his own limitations and those of his department's resources, he may imply that he is willing to try to do something far grander and more beneficial than he is able to do. At a policy level, this pretence is reflected in willingness of social services departments to take on responsibility for problems they cannot possibly solve, giving rise to expectations they cannot meet, and causing people to become either cynical and disillusioned, or else dependent on them in a way which is unrealistic, and which makes them more helpless and powerless than before.

It might be argued that in emphasising the social worker's need to be seen as helpful, I have underestimated the client's attempt to mislead him. The 'manipulative' client is a new and omnipresent stereotype in social work. He comes to the agency with the intention of deriving every possible material benefit by any available means. He will use threats or pleas, betray his dependants, revile his mother's memory, maim his children or sell his wife for the sake of exploiting the social worker's generosity. No trick is too low and no pretence too dishonest. I would suggest that this stereotype is largely the product of the naiveté I have been trying to describe. It is the counterpart to the picture I have drawn of the 'long-suffering' and 'tolerant' social worker who is so keen to help that he can see nothing but the material need, or the most obvious presenting symptom, of the client. It is when the social worker lacks sensitivity, subtlety and a complex understanding of the conflicting elements in a client's situation that deception occurs, and it is usually primarily self-deception by the social worker.

It is perfectly true that some clients do give misleading and incomplete accounts of themselves, and exert pressure on social workers to accomplish or prevent certain outcomes, often by material means. Very frequently these transactions are the products of repeated and unhelpful interventions by earlier social workers, so that the stereotypical client is actually a rehearsed version of a role that previous helpers have cast him in, playing to a script provided by his professional producers. Other clients are so desperate that they try to frighten or shame social workers into doing things for them. What they most need is to meet a social worker with the courage to get them to stop still for a moment, and reflect on the full implications of their position. Others still are driven by more powerful and primitive feelings, with which they overwhelm anyone who tries to help them. But the label 'manipulator' does these no justice at all. The force and terror of their emotions takes the social worker by storm, and he needs a firm grasp of his own perceptions and emotions to be able to give them any true help. Without this he is likely to be not so much manipulated as shipwrecked.

All these aspects of the professional social worker's task

will be developed in the next and subsequent chapters. What I have tried to show in this chapter is that such tasks are often dissociated from ordinary, friendly helping by a process closely related to the impulse to be naively helpful. While there is a real discipline and an important skill in professional help, its best basis lies in the subtlety and sensitivity that we employ to understand and deal with our own problems, and those of others close to us.

3
Worker and client

So far I have done little more than sketch in the background to the helping process in social work. I have tried to analyse the motives and attitudes of the helper, and their potential influence on that process. What I have not yet considered is the part played by the corresponding ideas and feelings of the person seeking help, or how the two parties' aspirations and emotional investments fuse together to produce an outcome. This chapter, therefore, is about how the helper and helped affect each other.

My first book, *Client-Worker Transactions*, was an attempt at doing this. It was written when I had been a probation officer for about four years, and was in many ways an account of my efforts to scramble over the barriers to my own development past a naive level of helping. But it was written largely in terms of my clients' influences on me, and as an attempt to make some sense of my often volatile and widely varied responses to specially deprived and self-destructive people. It did less than justice to my own contribution to those encounters, even though at the end of writing it I had far more insight into my part in the process than when I started.

What I tried to explore in the book was the way in which many clients seemed to ask for help, or use the help offered them, in an essentially defensive way, which precluded any real change in them or improvement in their circumstances. I argued that the principal way they did this was through the emotional effect they produced on the social worker. Being terrified of parts of themselves, of others near them or of their situations, they in turn terrified the social worker, not usually by direct threats or pleas, but more often by an unconscious process of influence. Their accounts of themselves and their circumstances were accompanied by an emotional splitting off of unwanted and disowned aspects of themselves, which acted powerfully on the social worker at a subterranean level. The effect of this process was quite marked, yet it was seldom recognised, because the social worker preferred to see himself as a balanced, clear-headed professional person, exercising scientific and objective judgments in the client's interests. Yet if he allowed himself to become aware of it, he was often uncomfortably conscious of a strong counter-current of primitive feelings inside himself – sometimes simultaneous and contradictory feelings of anger, despair, helplessness, dread and confusion. When he was honest enough to examine what most contributed to crucial decisions at crisis points, it was often these subterranean feelings more than his intellectual assessments.

I also suggested that this process of influence could only work through the social worker's own feelings being reinforced and exaggerated by the client's. Without an initial apprehensiveness, irritation or muddle in the worker, the emotional current transmitted from the client would not produce a reaction of this kind, still less a disproportionate or irrational one. Yet all social workers have feelings about such threatening and disruptive clients, and thus there is always some material for a transaction between them. The point is that the form of this transaction will depend on the worker's personality and defences as much as on the client's. The eventual outcome will reflect something about how both parties deal with strong infantile feelings. The worker cannot consciously control his emotional response to the client, nor should he try to do so. It represents a crucial indicator of what the client most needs help to overcome. His own feelings often show him the part of his problem that the client is least able to communicate verbally, yet most needs to share. So the worker should cultivate an ability to be in touch with his own reactions to the client, and to bring them into the foreground of his consciousness, rather than trying to repress them. He should learn how to play them back to the client in a constructive way, instead of attempting to deny and disown them, while actually being heavily influenced by them.

This is a very bald summary of the sort of understanding I tried to develop in that book. I hope in this one to show more fully how the social worker's notions of helping can have an important influence on the shape which such transactions take. In particular, I want to examine how they can sometimes contribute to unhelpful outcomes, and how these can be avoided.

Often the pattern of such unhelpful relationships is established at their very outset, particularly if first contact is in a crisis. Right at the start, sometimes in the first few seconds, the client communicates something at an emotional level which the social worker picks up and responds to in a certain way. Very often this transmission of a feeling to the worker is the key to a defensive manoeuvre by the client. The worker's response to it prevents him from reaching the 'middle' of the client, from getting to the essentials of his problem. He is thrown off course by the emotional impact of the transaction and left to deal with the disowned part of the client in himself. Unless he can recognise this, it will distort his reactions and affect the potential helpfulness of their relationship.

Presumably the social worker is trying from the outset to get to the essentials of the matter with which the client needs help by the shortest possible route. However necessary his concern, goodwill and desire to understand may be, they are not the purpose of the contact. He is there to be genuinely helpful, not just genuinely compassionate. The process I am trying to describe sometimes obscures this, and makes the social worker feel that he should do or be something because the client demands it, without really assessing the probable consequences, or the likelihood of his actions being any real help.

It ought to be possible to achieve a direct route to the client's real needs for help simply by good listening, and it usually is. But in the sort of examples of this process I have in mind, things are not so straightforward. I have been struck by the extremes to which I have been driven in order to combat what I experienced as defensive manoeuvres by clients, or as exploitation of my situation as a 'sitting duck' whom they could misuse by provoking unhelpful reactions. Usually I have recognised this because in one or more instances I have gone along with what was demanded or more subtly expected of me, and the outcome has been disastrous. Often I have done what was required by the client because it all too easily fulfilled my own naive stereotype of helpfulness as well as his misleading one.

Two very common examples of stereotypical 'help' which is sometimes unhelpful are those of giving people things and listening to their problems. At a naive level, these are just the sort of things that social workers are supposed to do, and often can do helpfully. But for some clients, the demand for things or for passive listening is based on a defensive manoeuvre in which, if the social worker responds according to the stereotype, he is experienced as being not compassionate but rejecting, not helping but hindering. In order to break out of this kind of transaction, he needs to recognise what is propelling him towards his response, both from the client's emotional pressure, and from his own naive and blinkered notion of help.

The best example I have experienced of the first kind of situation is still the one I gave in the first chapter of *Client-Worker Transactions.* I have not reacted in the same way since because my client, Mr Peterson, taught me a lesson which I have never forgotten. Briefly, what happened was that he came as a casual caller to the office where I had just started work, but where he was well known. He demanded money in a drunken, aggressive, threatening way, and he was a big, tough-looking man. He had just come out of prison, and told an improbable story about wanting to travel to work in the next town. He hinted that if he did not get the money he would commit a further offence to return to prison. I gave him the small sum of money he demanded, but was uncomfortably half-aware that I was acting in bad faith. My motives were largely cowardice and evasion of the true issue. I was really giving him money to get rid of him, not to help him. So when I heard the following day that he had in fact committed another petty crime, and been sent to prison,

I felt very guilty. I suspected that it was not so much in spite of my 'help' as because of it. I resolved not to do this again. When he came in again to demand money soon after serving his sentence, I told him I would try to help in any other way I could – specially over his need for a home – but I would not give him money. He was at first incredulous, then contemptuous, scornful, furious, explosive. What did I possibly imagine I, a miserable beginner, could do for him? How dare I refuse him what others, my elders and betters, had always given? What sort of probation officer did I think I was? I stuck as calmly as I could to an explanation of my view that giving him money would not help, but that I would try to do anything else in my power. In the end, after I had thought he was going to attack me, he settled for having a bath at the public conveniences, and I accompanied him there to pay for it. On the way (and I seem to have censored this in my account in *Client-Worker Transactions*) he made a raucous scene, calculated to shame me in front of everyone in the street and in the lavatories. He accused me of every folly of youth and inexperience, shouting my incompetence to passers-by. We had what was practically a stand-up fight in the Gents, in front of startled onlookers. But he returned from his bath to apologise and thank me. Soon afterwards he came back yet again, having not been in further trouble, and I spent nearly the whole of a rain-soaked week with him, searching for accommodation. We found a temporary address, from which he moved to a permanent one, which he found for himself, with help from a church voluntary worker. This was the start of a nine-year period during which I continued to see Mr Peterson, weekly or fortnightly, drunk or sober, at his house or mine, in the street or the pub, at all hours of day and night, in various states of exaltation or collapse. He assumed the status of a kind of eccentric and unreliable uncle to my children, gave them presents, came to tea. He got into minor bits of trouble, but kept out of prison – something he had not managed to do for more than a few months at a time during the previous ten years or more. Sadly, he drifted back into his old life-style when I left the probation service, but I have since heard that he has settled again, and has been out of prison for the past two years.

The lesson I learnt from my original mistake with Mr Peterson was that some people can only ask for help in a form which, though apparently stereotypically right and reasonable to expect of a social worker, for them constitutes rejection. Mr Peterson's request for help stemmed from feeling despairing, helpless, lost and childlike. He frightened me so much by these feelings (not by his physical threats) that I rejected him. I did so by giving him what he was asking for, but what I knew in my heart to be a symbol of rejection. I was buying peace and quiet, and he knew it. He was able to make me feel that no true help was possible, so that my actions confirmed his worst fears. When I realised what I had done, I was able to challenge this assumption. My new attitude made him angry and confused, but not for very long. He soon recognised that my refusing to give him false help was symbolically an offer of true help. He came back to test out the genuineness of this offer, and for nine years he was not disappointed.

I want to make it very clear that I am not suggesting that social workers should never give clients money or material help. During those years I gave Mr Peterson innumerable meals (I ate with him), clothes (especially underpants) and sheets. But I would not give him money because of what it represented – getting rid of him. I often helped him get money from Social Security, because that had no such symbolic significance for him. What matters here is not some general rule about which welfare agency or profession should give what to whom (though important issues of rights are often at stake in such transactions), it is a question of good faith. Is the social worker being asked to do something that he knows in his heart to fulfil a covert purpose, quite different from the apparent one, and much less helpful? There may be some excuse for going along with such a transaction once with a client, but there is really none for doing it over and over again.

The second kind of example is more familiar to me from my recent psychiatric experience. It consists in unhelpfully 'listening to problems', where the client's talk has become an empty recital and repetition of a hackneyed history or a series of clichés. This happened to me quite often in my early months at the mental hospital. At first I was slightly flattered and gratified by clients' willingness to confide so early in their meetings with me, often in first interviews. It seemed like a nice change after the inarticulate mutterings of hostile probationers and prisoners. But I quickly became aware of how hollow these confidences could be, and that even listening to them might be unhelpful. In sitting there I was by implication confirming my status as yet another 'helpful' person whose unhelpfulness lay in the process of passive, compliant willingness to hear these meaningless noises. Once again, the transaction was one of bad faith. The client was often telling me, non-verbally, that there was no way I was going to help him. He was giving me a covert message that there was nothing I or anybody could do for him. By just sitting there, passively listening, I was agreeing with him.

As a rather extreme example of my refusal to accept this role on occasions, I shall give an account of my first meeting with Beryl Flanagan. She was a patient in her fifties, with a long history of psychiatric treatment in hospital and outside, who had just been admitted to the ward. She asked to see me, and as she left a group of fellow-patients she made a facetious remark about 'turning on the tape-recorder'. On entering my room, she sat down, shut her eyes, and launched into a monologue about her complicated financial affairs (not apparently directly related to her admission), pointing occasionally to a large wicker bag full of papers which seemed to be about these matters. After about ten minutes of this I began to feel very restless and rather angry. I realised that there was no way in which I could interrupt the flow of her emotionless, rambling account. Since I do not follow the social work fashion of emitting noises like 'Yes', 'Quite', or 'Mm', at intervals, I was sitting in silence. As she had her eyes closed, my stony expression was lost on her. I began to think of ways I could communicate to her the effects she was having on me and had, I suspected, on others she met. I got quietly out of my chair and moved around to the other side of the desk by whch she was sitting, and stood with my back to the wall. She continued to tell her story to the empty chair. After a few more moments, I sat on the floor behind the desk, now completely out of sight of her. She went on talking. I waited a little, then shouted, 'STOP' in the middle of one of her sentences. She must have opened her eyes, for she sounded surprised to find I had gone. Still sitting on the floor out of sight, I explained to her that I had retreated to this position to show her what she made me feel like doing. She sounded confused and rather angry about this. I explained that she made me feel she was not behaving like a human being, or treating me as a human being either. I thought we should end the interview at that point and start again next time on an entirely different basis, each trying to find ways of acknowledging the other as human. She became angrier, and said she hadn't finished explaining her problem. I told her politely but firmly that this interview was over, but that I would be glad to see her again two days later. When I showed her out of the room, she burst into floods of tears, and said with real despair that she felt like killing herself. She knew she bored people and drove them away from her. Sobbing, she said that everything I said was true, but she felt helpless to do anything about it. For a further half an hour we stood in the corridor while she cried and talked very feelingly about her real problems. I arranged to come in specially to see her the next day. I went back in a state of some anxiety, wondering what this had done to her, afraid that I might have been too brutal. She looked quite different, much more vital, bright and lively. She talked with her eyes open, facing me. Her wicker bag was almost empty, and she hardly referred to it. She thanked me very much for helping her, and started to talk about leaving hospital and beginning a new life. She said she had needed to be told the truth, and I was the first person to face her with it for years. She left hospital the next week, and I have seen her twice in the nine months since then, and had a few telephone converstions with her. She took a job, bought a house and started a business. She has not been near a mental hospital or a psychiatrist since then, and says she is better than she has been for years.

The directness of my expression of what I felt Beryl was doing to me in our first meeting was partly made possible by the mental hospital setting. Nursing staff had told me a bit about her (mainly that in view of her record of admissions they feared that she might be difficult to motivate to leave the hospital). Also, after the interview, I was in a position to alert the nurses to the fact that Beryl was genuinely distressed, so that she could have a further opportunity to talk about her real feelings with them when I left. The main fear I might otherwise have had (probably unrealistically) was of having abandoned her in a very vulnerable state, with a consequent risk of suicide. But if these features of the protected hospital setting made this rather extreme action possible, my determination to avoid the bad faith of sitting listening to Beryl's recital seemed to have been justified. There are other, less dramatic and sudden, ways of getting to the essentials which are more suited to other settings. I often ask clients to act out feelings, to show me what they *do* when feeling something, or to 'become' different aspects of themselves, rather than tell lifeless stories or list problems.

The common theme in these two examples seemed to be a refusal by the social worker to take a 'leap of bad faith' with the client. Both initial approaches invited or drove me towards a response which conformed with an apparently reasonable expectation, but at the expense of truth to my feelings. The clue to the real help they needed lay not in the conventional social work reaction but in my own covert emotions, of despair in one case and anger in the other. It later emerged that Mr Peterson felt every bit as miserable and hopeless as he made me feel, while Beryl was really very angry with all the 'helpers' who had done nothing to help her. (Before leaving the hospital, she took a day out to travel to London and confront her private psychotherapist with the fact that for two years he had been wasting her time and money.) Thus by acting upon what they did to me rather than what they asked me to do, I seemed to be able to reach an acknowledgment and sharing of their real pain, rather than become a part of their unsuccessful defence against it.

In addition to these difficulties in escaping from stereotypical responses, the social worker also has to overcome his tendency to place his own limits on the client's pain. I have already mentioned how hard it can be to let people tell their own stories and reach their own conclusions. It is especially difficult to allow a really troubled client to tell the worst, to say which aspect of his situation is most unbearable for him, and share his feelings about it. This is a difficulty in all kinds of helping, but in professional social work it is exaggerated by a sort of tacit assumption that the social worker should be able to 'solve clients' problems', or at least help the client identify and manage them. It tempts the social worker to put boundaries and definitions around what the client is saying in a premature and clumsy attempt at helping. It leads to the worker adopting the role of an artificial barrier between the client and what is worst for him. This protective role is a defensive collusion between social worker and client, in the face of problems of enormous proportions or feelings of alarming ferocity, or complexities and bewildering contradictions. It prevents the real sharing which alone permits true help.

This is another example of a joint defence in which the client's fears trigger off a reaction from the worker which stems from his naive motivation to be helpful. There is something in the motivation of every social worker (as there was in my own) which gives a strong desire to be in control of the forces or feelings at whose mercy the client seems to be. Added to this is a wish to become *responsible* for his situation, in order to make it happier and better for him. Presumably this naive desire to take control and responsibility away from people who feel frightened and helpless is again an uncritical carry-over from the experience of being a child in relation to adults, and especially parents. At a certain point in the client's account of his situation, the worker feels a strong urge to say, 'Enough', and on the basis of his incomplete journey into the client's world, start to make offers of himself and his agency's resources, to map and plan and fence off the territory of his problem. He picks up the client's distress as be begins to get near the most difficult facts and feelings, rushes past him, and turns him back towards the safer ground he has already crossed. Like an anxious parent, he forbids exploration of the dark and dreaded areas of fear and danger.

This is unhelpful because it diverts the client from his attempt to reach some expression of what is worst for him and in sharing it, to discover for himself whether he can face it, and how much responsibility he can take for bearing it. If the worker takes control and responsibility away from him, there can be no true sharing of what is most feared, and this largely confirms the client's worst fears that he is quite unfit to handle his problems. It interrupts his attempt to make some sense of his muddles and panics, and gives him the message that he needs the social worker to do this and more for him.

I vividly remember as a very young probation officer my first experience of someone who refused to be deflected from his determination to tell me the worst, in spite of anything I might try to do to stop him. One winter's afternoon a middle-aged man walked into the office and said he had to tell me about the trouble he was in. He started on an incredibly complex account of his personal and business life, full of broken relationships, financial ruins, shady deals and cruel disappointments. After an hour he was only up to 1949, and I had another appointment. He insisted on seeing me again, saying I would see where he was leading eventually. This happened a second time, and a third. Only in the fourth appointment did his relentless account of calamities end, with his own summary of a disastrous situation, in which he faced imprisonment for bankruptcy offences and fraud, leaving behind a young wife, with one small child and expecting another, and a mountain of unpaid debts. But his repeated theme was that he had spent half a lifetime running away from the most sordid and unpalatable aspects of his story, and that no one, least of all me, was going to stop him telling the truth this once, and facing up to his past, for the sake of his future. His determination impressed me greatly, and it took him through his inevitable sentence, through many disappointments after it, and on to a better future for himself and his family once these had been endured.

Years later in the mental hospital, I met a man with a very similar history, who had got himself into a very similar financial mess. The difference was that he was much less willing to face the awfulness of the mess or the consequences of his actions. In particular, he wanted to dwell on the details and his feelings about a recently broken marriage rather than the realities of his financial disasters. He referred to them, but then slid away again. I had to hold him to the task of facing the facts of a series of frauds and other offences for which he might be imprisoned; I also had to insist that these were not the consequences of mental illness as he suggested. It was no easy matter for him to admit this to himself, to leave hospital and face a life of poverty alone. Yet in the end he did all this and gave himself up to the police for the offences; and then so successfully rehabilitated himself before the court hearing that he avoided imprisonment by paying back all his creditors.

In the first example, the client's determination overcame my resistance to hearing his whole story; in the second, taking my inspiration mainly from the first client, I helped the second man overcome his fear of the worst in his circumstances. Most clients in a terrible mess fall somewhere between these two; they are ambivalent about the worst. They invite protection and diversion from what they most fear, yet once the worker becomes aware of his own resistance to allowing them to share it, they can readily be helped to do so. If the worker has a firm grasp of the importance of getting right to the essentials, the client can draw strength from this.

What the second example shows is that the worker does sometimes have a responsibility for guiding the client towards an acknowledgment of what is least bearable for him. Where he senses that the client is being evasive and misleading, as in this case, he can helpfully take some control over the direction of their conversation, and be responsible for steering him towards what he senses to be the dangerous area. But this element of control is for the opposite purpose from the one I was earlier criticising. It is used in the earliest stages, not to limit the definition of the problem territory, but to widen and deepen it. The art of helping such people seems to lie in giving up much of this responsibility and control just when the client feels most threatened. When the second man acknowledged that he had lost everything and that he risked a prison sentence, he desperately tried to get me to adopt the protective rôle of an advocate and conciliator on his behalf, with doctors, solicitors and everyone else. When I refused to do this, he was angry and non-plussed. I felt terribly guilty as he wept and shook defencelessly like a cornered animal.

He made me feel as if I was a merciless persecutor who had hunted him down and taken away all his armour. Yet slowly he recognised that what I was offering him was a relationship based on genuine respect for his many good qualities – creativity, kindness, generosity and intelligence – which would have been impossible if I had been part of his protective screen against his weaknesses. I could only get alongside him if I refused to be a guardian over him. When he had allowed me to see him in his most vulnerable state, without his shell, and found that I was not panicked by his helplessness, not driven to shelter him, he found that he too could bear his vulnerability. It was as if the mere fact of displaying his worst self and having it recognised by somebody else, who was neither repelled nor moved to protective pity, was partly cathartic. He discovered that he was not quite as bad as he feared, though he realised this for himself, not as a result of my reassurance. The true reassurance lay in the fact that I had not been destroyed or alienated, and I was willing to go on seeing him. My refusal to take away any of his responsibility and control over his life was a vote of confidence in him. There were many times when I feared that I was expecting too much of him, when I left him alone and miserable in his flat. Yet his decision to give himself up to the police – which eventually saved him from prison – was entirely his own, and took me by surprise. It showed that he was even more worthy of my respect than I had realised.

However hard clients sometimes press social workers to place artificial limits round their problems, there are always dangers in social workers taking on this role. At best, it can provide only an immediate, short-term relief. Where the social worker decides it is necessary, or finds he has been pushed into doing it, he should immediately start looking for ways of handing responsibility and control back to the client again, or at least sharing them with him. It is, after all, his life. Sooner or later, he will become frustrated with the artificiality and ineffectiveness of the protection he is getting from the social worker. Either the worker will not be able to sustain the role, or the client will recognise the bad faith implicit in it. He will see that the relationship is not based on respect, but on anxiety about what has never been faced or shared between them. He will see that the worker is no more able and willing to face the worst than he is. Accordingly, the client will begin to test the worker out, as his own worst fears re-emerge. This will reveal the fragility of a defensive relationship, built upon a basis of falseness.

I am suggesting that the worker should always try to share problems with the client, not usurp or annex parts of the client's life. Yet sometimes clients really cannot deal with their problems. At a moment of crisis, they need someone to intervene, to take over, rescue them or others from them, and to put them in another, safer situation. In this particular set of circumstances, this is the only help they can accept, and the only kind a social worker can appropriately give them.

I do not for a moment want to suggest that such crises do not occur, or that social workers do not have a vital part to play in them. In the next chapter, I shall try to outline some notions of how to recognise these true crises, and how the social worker should try to act in them. What I do want to suggest is that there is a strong tendency for social workers to over-estimate the incidence of these crises, particularly when they involve clients who are unfamiliar. (In the next chapter I shall argue that they may similarly *under*-estimate the seriousness of some situations when they have been working with clients for a long time.)

The social worker in a statutory agency has the role of official gate-keeper to such residential institutions as mental hospitals, hostels, children's homes and old people's homes. He is seen by some people in difficulties as the municipal guardian of these protective resources, who holds the key to their problems because he can take away a very difficult person and keep him safely elsewhere. On many occasions, the pressure on the social worker to react in drastic and often unhelpful ways in a 'crisis' stems from the fact that the client is not his case. The social worker on night or weekend duty is often presented with apparently life-and-death situations which demand drastic remedies but which, if he knew the family better, might quite easily be resolved between them. The worker's problem is that it is far easier for the family to treat a stranger as a stereotypical offical, whose job is to impose a standard, 'logical' solution to a situation which 'obviously' needs it, than it is to do the same with a person who is known and who knows the family, including the difficult member, in other roles and circumstances. It is correspondingly more difficult for the duty social worker to assert his own human, non-official values and perceptions.

It is a frustratingly unreal feeling to find oneself talking about the most intimate and painful areas of a family's life, yet doing so in an emotional climate in which one is cast in the role of local authority agent, called to impose a standard official resolution of the conflict. In such circumstances, it can seem to the social worker as if he has no right to be humanly honest, let alone personal. He feels as if he cannot react in the way an ordinary person might behave – becoming angry, or expressing compassion or concern for the alleged deviant. The family is very convincing in its insistence on receiving this very personal kind of assistance in an impersonal way.

Unfortunately, a combination of pressure of work and lack of confidence in some statutory social work agencies has led to much social work being in the 'crisis intervention' style which is forced upon weekend and night duty workers. It can even come to be the case that social workers see their everyday role in almost the same impersonal and stereotypical way as the kind of family I have just described see it. They come to recognise an impersonal intervention, to remove or rescue, as being the major or even the sole purpose of social work. The notion that social workers should always be trying to share with clients, to help on as nearly an equal basis of responsibility as possible, has become quite foreign in some departments. Thus again there can be an unhelpful collusion between the defensive expectations of the clients and the restrictive self-image of the social worker.

The pattern set by such interventions can be long-lasting. Clients and their families can come to see residential establishments as places of refuge to which they can occasionally or frequently resort as an escape from dilemmas and conflicts, so that when in difficulties their first thought is of a possible admission. When this pattern has been set by the way earlier social workers have handled similar events, it becomes very difficult for a new social worker to persuade the clients of the possibility of dealing with their situation in some other way. It may take quite a lot of courage to challenge the clients' expectations of him. If they have always encountered a willingness, even an eagerness, in earlier social workers to play safe by organising an admission (of an adult to mental hospital or a child into care, for instance) then they are likely to react to a new social worker's resistance to this solution with shock and disbelief. They may question his experience, his competence, his judgment, his humanity and occasionally even his sanity. They may make him feel very threatened and exposed. Whatever doubts he previously had about their ability to withstand the stress of the crisis, their capacity to take a greater degree of responsibility for holding onto a difficult situation, these doubts will be redoubled. It will be a real test of his nerve and persistence if he is to go on requiring of them what he judges to be a measure of strength of which they are capable.

In these circumstances, it is particularly difficult for the social worker not to become tense and defensive. He may feel angry about the pressure which is being put on him, yet unable to express this directly, because it seems inappropriate. He may feel that what is being asked of him is unjustified and unreasonable, yet find it hard to put this across to the client except in a series of objections, starting, 'Yes, but . . . ', or of counterproposals in the form, 'Don't you think you could try . . .'. These tend to be experienced by the clients as typically official reactions to requests for provision of resources – a form of bureaucratic blocking once described as 'goalkeeping'. Often this is not what the social worker is trying to do, but the oddly impersonal quality of the whole transaction seems to prevent him from expressing his feelings of concern, and his doubts about the real help which the client will derive from his doing what is expected of him.

Recently I was called out at a weekend to see a patient, Margaret Thompson, who had been discharged from the mental hospital two days previously, and had already taken an overdose. She had been admitted to the general hospital to be pumped out, and then sent home. I felt very unsure about my visit, because although she had been on my ward, I had had no contact with her during her two months in hospital, nor could I get hold of those who had been seeing her. I found her in a rather pathetic state, looking tense and stiff, complaining of being unable to bear her overwhelming feelings of destructiveness. In particular, she felt swamped by a desire to hurt or kill her two young children, and it was this that had caused her to take the overdose. Her husband Jack was a calm, patient man, who was doing all the real caring for the children, and keeping a very close eye on her, but he was obviously frustrated that things should have gone wrong so quickly, when he had been holding the fort for eight weeks on his own. Margaret never actually asked to come back into hospital, but she kept begging me to help her, and to take away the feelings that were plaguing her. I felt under strong pressure to arrange her readmission, especially as I had such a slim knowledge of her as a basis for any alternative help. But the nursing staff who had told me of her overdose felt strongly that she had derived little benefit from being in hospital, and that having her back would be a retrograde step.

It is tempting in such circumstances not to mention the possibility of an admission at all, and to hope that the client can be diverted into some alternative. But with someone making such dark threats – child-battering *and* suicide – such a strategy would be likely to be disastrous. It might have given Margaret the impression that I hadn't heard the despairing part of her message, and have driven her to even more destructive actions. So I asked Margaret and Jack directly whether she wanted to come back to hospital. This enabled them to discuss the pros and cons quite rationally for a time. It seemed to give them a feeling that I regarded the situation as not so drastic and urgent that I had to make a decision for them, and Jack in particular was able to voice his doubts about what would be gained by a readmission, saying Margaret hadn't really given herself a chance to try things out yet. After some sensible discussion, I arranged to visit again during the weekend. The second time, although she was still complaining about feelings of wanting to hurt the children, she seemed less frightened, and I was able to get her and

Jack to do a number of simple exercises designed to reduce her fears still further. She used a teddy bear as the baby, and rehearsed feeding it, describing her feelings as she did so. She and Jack reversed roles, and she was able to smile and relax as she listened to his excellent impersonation of her anxious self, and to try to reassure him. We also made a hierarchy of the tasks she feared, from going outside the house to being left alone with the children, and she and Jack agreed to work through the list gradually, one task at a time. By the end of this visit, she was strongly rejecting the idea of going back to hospital.

However, when I visited again in the middle of the following week, she greeted me more feebly and complainingly than ever, holding her head, staggering about, and begging for help. She said that her ideas of hurting the children had receded, but she felt dizzy and strange, and she couldn't stand it a moment longer. After we had talked about this for some time, and she still urged me to take the feelings away, I pointed out that I felt under strong pressure from her to get her back into hospital. I reminded her that we had discussed this at the weekend, that Jack had hoped it could be avoided, and that the hospital staff very much doubted they could help her. When she still insisted that she needed relief from her feelings, and kept repeating, 'Help me, help me', I said that if she wanted to go back to hospital, she must make that decision. I was not going to decide for her, or to pretend that I thought it was helpful to take her back there. Only she knew whether she could stand her anxiety about her everyday life and responsibilities, but I certainly did not belive I would be helping her to remove her from them. I also doubted whether Jack's patience would last for another long admission, after this one had produced so little progress. When Jack came in he confirmed this, and Margaret gradually calmed down, and eventually said she would try again. By the weekend she was doing well with her list of difficult tasks, and in the following interview she said she was glad that I had not given in to her pressure, and felt ashamed at having behaved so tiresomely. She wanted to try to get better as quickly as possible so that Jack could return to work, and they could live a normal life again. (Within three months this was, in fact, achieved. Jack is working, Margaret is leading an active social life, and they no longer need a social worker).

Because Margaret had had several previous admissions to hospital, she had come to see this as a way of dealing with the discomforts of emotional conflicts. By then Jack had become very sceptical of the value of the treatment she was receiving, but he was too diffident to express this directly. If Margaret had been readmitted, he would probably have taken unilateral action, making other arrangements for his future without reference to the hospital. Margaret herself was ambivalent, but she only knew one way of asking for help, which was a more or less direct plea to come back as an in-patient. When Margaret was at her most desperate, the turning point seemed to come through my pointing out the pressure she put me under to do something I felt to be unhelpful. I insisted on my right to my opinion that this would not help, and made her take responsibility for the decision, if she was to return to the hospital. This seemed to allow the other side of her feelings to resurface. From being like a helpless, pathetic child she became more adult and balanced, as she had before when I asked her if she wanted to go to hospital. By refusing to act as if the decision was mine to take for her – when in fact I would have been doing no more than rubber-stamping her emotional blackmail if I had arranged an admission – I was able to involve first her and then her husband in a more appropriate and helpful way of tackling the real difficulties they faced together.

When people like Margaret are in the grip of stressful and upsetting events, they become so afraid of the destructiveness of their fantasies that they lose sight of other dimensions of their lives. The personal and moral issues of their situation can be, and often are, completely overlooked. The presence of a social worker can actually make it easier to ignore obligations to others, to forget the importance of emotional ties and the needs of children. The possible evil effects, and the long-term damage to relationships of certain courses of action can fade from view, in face of some overwhelming dread. The discussion starts to be about how much stress someone can bear, how normal or abnormal someone else's behaviour is, what treatment another requires. It is as if the presence of a social worker allows human considerations to be suspended, and substitutes morally neutral criteria, on a quasi-medical model, by which he will judge what outcomes are best, and how to produce them.

Frequently, therefore, the social worker's task in resisting pressures for admissions which he judges to be inappropriate and unnecessary is the reintroduction of moral and human criteria into the discussion of the crisis. He needs to find some way of asserting the claims of the personal and the relational, rather than the pseudo-psychological or the medical. Sometimes an exhausted and frustrated family can appear to have forgotten that their very difficult handicapped child or their dementing grandparent is really a human being, and one of their family. It is a very delicate task to bring them back to this notion in a way which does not sound reproachful or pharisaical.

There are several different ways in which this can be attempted. If the social worker is trying to restore the family to its sense of these priorities, he needs to make it clear that he places a positive view on these attributes of relationships. He needs to recognise with them that it is very difficult indeed to retain love, loyalty, compassion and kindness in the circumstances that such families endure, but that these standards are of worth in themselves, and that he himself is trying to uphold them. He needs to make it clear that he realises that it may be an exceptional level of tolerance and patience that is being required, but that he believes that it is well worth struggling to achieve this, and that the good that may be accomplished is worth the very considerable effort. He needs to give proof of his willingness not only to recognise but to share their pain in their circumstances. He should try to treat them as he hopes they will treat each other, and to set an example in consideration, sensitivity and openness to their needs.

However, in some circumstances this gentle approach can be ineffective. Sometimes people demand protection from themselves or each other in a way which is subtly evasive of the true issues between them. They attempt to involve the worker in their defences of themselves and their deceptions of each other, or simply in obscuring the moral realities of their relationships. In such instances the social worker may have little alternative but to adopt a very firm stance, insisting on some point as being of crucial importance, and holding them to the pain of considering it. This is a much more didactic approach than the one just described, and one in which the blunt and solid assertion of what seems both real and important to the social worker is the only available key to a consideration of the moral issues by the clients in crisis.

I found myself recently in such a situation. Mary, a widow in her forties, had been admitted to the hospital with many problems. Since her husband's death five years previously she had been subject to increasingly severe attacks of panic and disorientation. She had reached a point of remaining in bed for most of the day, weeping a good deal. She had lost control of her very bright and lively teenage son, who was stealing and truanting from school. She remained in hospital for several months, and seemed to benefit greatly from the opportunity to re-examine these issues, individually and in groups, and to work towards a much more positive attitude to her relationships and responsibilities. She did very well on discharge, and soon re-established herself in a job, and in an affectionate but realistic control over her son. However, when he left home to start work some months later, her old pattern of panic and retreat began to re-emerge. For some time she had had a friendship with an older man who had himself received mental hospital treatment some years earlier. He was very concerned and protective towards her, constantly solicitous of her wellbeing. He started to spend more and more time with her, until he was a constant companion; yet she grew, if anything, worse. I had been visiting her ever since she left hospital, and eventually she confided in me that she had become very frustrated with her whole way of life. She found that in the company of her friend (Roger) she was often bored, and longed to be able to be more lively, adventurous, youthful and free. Yet such was her fear of herself that she needed him constantly to be present, as she felt she was in danger otherwise of killing herself. She now felt that Roger was taking advantage of her weakness, as he was pressurising her to let him live with her. She said she was not committed to her relationship with him, and she seemed very ambivalent about their mutual dependence. She saw his moving in as symbolic of a permanent attachment, and said that she did not want this to happen. She agreed with my suggestion that there was no way that she could be in a position to try to achieve greater autonomy, and to take more initiatives to meet new people and go to new places, if she allowed Roger to play the role of nurse and companion. Yet she was not willing to follow up practical suggestions I made about alternative ways of feeling safe without being tied to Roger – such as staying for a time with other friends she had made in hospital. She did acknowledge that what she mainly needed was the courage to risk her life, in order to have a life of her own.

The next time I visited her I found Roger in close attendance, and they announced that he had moved in. Mary betrayed nothing in her expression as she told me this news, and made no attempt to see me on her own. She was neither much better, nor much worse. When they both expressed some concern over how her son might react to the news of his encampment there, I tried to get them to tell me straightforwardly how they saw their relationship, and how they intended to describe it to him. Roger still insisted that he was 'looking after' Mary, and concerned only for her welfare, implicitly denying both a sexual relationship, and that his own needs were being met in any way. Mary gave no sign of wanting to contradict his account, and I felt that they were both essentially hypocritical and untruthful in what they said. I doubted the value of my visiting her further as I felt it impossible to have an honest discussion. However, I did not say this to them then.

The following month, on the evening I was due to visit again, I was very much delayed at the hospital, and telephoned to suggest that I might postpone my visit to another night. Roger answered the phone, and I explained that I was both late and tired. However, he insisted that Mary was in a very bad state, and implored me to come. I agreed, resolved to take the bull by the horns, had a stiff drink, and set out, through a storm, at a rather fast pace. I found Roger fussing over a tearful, huddled, downcast and dishevelled

Mary. He said that she needed treatment very urgently, that her previous admission had not got to the root of the problem; that he was not pressing for readmission, but some form of deep psychotherapy. After a while, I stopped Roger's rather tremulous flow and asked him to answer two questions. The first was, 'What is the purpose of your life?' He replied, at once, 'To look after Mary'. I then asked, 'And what is the purpose of her life?', and he replied, equally quickly, that she did not have one. I suggested that this was their problem. I pointed out that Mary sat around all day, waited upon by him, never left alone for a minute, yet she was more frightened and lonely than ever. She was suffering quite simply from a meaningless life. Mary looked up at this, but went on crying. Roger begged to disagree, and pointed out that she had many things to occupy her, but when I challenged him to name any of significance he had some difficulty in doing so. I suggested that they had made of themselves a safe and comfortable prison, and that now Mary felt trapped in it, and Roger, for all his kindness, was her jailer. He denied this, saying he had encouraged her to get 'a little job, helping some old ladies run a charity shop'. I wondered why he had not encouraged her to be a night club hostess, or to join a trans-antarctic expedition. She was young, attractive, and healthy, and had no ties. Why was he so limited in his aspirations for her? Roger still insisted that I was wrong. He then played his trump card. He said he could prove that her symptoms were not caused by the factors I mentioned, because she had got in a similar state when her husband was alive. Taking my courage in my hands, I said that I thought this meant that her life was meaningless then too. At this Mary sat up, and remained upright, looking at me, but not angrily. I then addressed myself to her. I suggested that what she was feeling was not depression but fear. I said I thought she was obsessed by ideas of death, feeling both fascinated and attracted by the idea of death, but also terrified of dying. She nodded her agreement. I said I thought she felt like this because of all the potential in her that was not being used. She was potentially a strong and forthright person, who had a lot to give other people, and who was capable of being an active, vigorous and contributing member of the community.

I reminded her of some occasions when I had seen her act courageously and unselfishly, in moments of crisis over her son. I said I thought she had a great deal to offer, but that she was afraid to risk losing the security of her present situation, and the very safe boundaries she had put around herself. I thought both she and Roger were using each other in a way which was unfair on both of them and which was distorting and dishonest. Her life was meaningless because she put meaningless limits on it. She resented these limits, including the ones in Roger's imagination of what she could do and be, but she was not willing to risk breaking out of them. However, if she did not, she would remain unhappy, frustrated and afraid for the rest of her life. During all this, Mary looked more and more alive, alert and interested. She had stopped crying, acknowledged my points, and made some of her own. Eventually, I said I knew that I had been brusque and somewhat brutal, insisted that my stance was based on a real concern about what they were doing to each other and themselves, and left. I was pretty anxious afterwards that I had overdone my confrontation with them, but I fought off the temptation to ring up to check that they were still alive, as I recognised that this would simply be an attempt to allay my own anxiety. Eventually, after about six weeks, I telephoned to offer to visit them again. Mary answered the phone in a firm and cheerful voice, and told me that ever since my visit she had been getting better. She had in fact started a new job that morning. She made no comment about Roger, but said that she had resolved to tackle her life in a different spirit, and that she had been making real progress in overcoming her fears. She hoped that she would not need to see me, or a psychiatrist again, but she was glad of the help she had received.

In this example, my aggressiveness with Mary and Roger was partly the result of my previous failure to communicate to them the discomfort I felt at what seemed dishonest in their relationship, and above all in the way they were using me. When they told me Roger had moved in, I felt that they were not being straight with each other or with me. I felt that Mary had chosen to confide her doubts about her relationship with Roger to me, but now was choosing to tell me that she had done what she said she would not do in such a way as to make it very difficult for me to remind her of those doubts. Yet she was not renouncing her previous reservations either. The result was that I had a feeling of being bound hand and foot, of being made unable to be of any help to them. So when Roger asked me, rather unreasonably, to come urgently to see them, I was very angry. I knew that at least part of the origin of Mary's misery was precisely what she had covertly forbidden me to discuss in front of Roger, and I suspected that he, too, sensed this. The only way of breaking out of the bind they had put me in was to be extremely direct in challenging them.

Obviously, my own style of dealing with this sort of situation would not suit everyone, and has evolved from the sort of person I am in other aspects of my life. All the examples given in this chapter have shown the social worker taking a rather strong line, refusing to be passive and compliant, to fit in with conventional expectations of the helpful official. What I want to emphasise is that this did not simply take the form of resistance to unreasonable pressure. In every case I indicated to the client what he was doing to me at an emotional level. I tried to bring out into the open the very strong undercurrent of feeling in what was happening between us, so that we could both look at the *real* transaction, rather than get hung up on the pseudo-issues of a verbal battle. This attempt to make explicit the truth of what was really going on seemed to be recognisable to the client as an effort to establish more real and meaningful communications between us. The fact that I was able to offer him back what he did to me – even sometimes in an angry way – appeared to make our relationship more real and personal. It allowed contact to be made between the 'middle' of him and the 'middle' of myself, or rather it allowed this to be made overt, rather than subterranean. Instead of the covert terrorisation of the social worker by an unacknowledged process of emotional pressures, we were able to reach a sharing of every aspect of the problem, including what was most feared.

Unless some such approach is adopted, I think there is a risk of social work being used as part of the defensive screen which all of us occasionally try to put between ourselves and the real dilemmas of our lives. Social workers often meet people facing appalling conflicts of interests, of loyalties, of feelings. Such people experience painful ambivalence about growing and changing, about risking something of themselves to resolve these conflicts. The social worker is often a stranger, an unknown quantity, and often also a last resort. No wonder clients invite a response which is unhelpful, in the sense that it tends to consolidate on their entrenched position, rather than seize an opportunity for change. It is for the social worker to prove that he is strong and reliable enough to help the client cross the barriers to his development.

I hope I have not given the impression that I think this can be done suddenly, dramatically and once-for-all. My contact with nearly all the people described in this chapter was over a number of months, and in several of them over many years. What I am suggesting is that it may be necessary for the social worker to take a determined stand, often right at the start of the relationship, if he is to prove helpful. In this way, he can clear the ground for the sensitivity and good listening, the empathy and compassion, that I tried to describe in the previous chapter.

4 Compulsion and supervision

Some of the people that a social worker sees have not asked for his help. People who break the law, who suffer from serious mental illnesses, or who maltreat their children are usually referred to social workers by other officials (police, doctors) or by neighbours. In all such circumstances, social workers will play an important part in deciding what should happen to these people, and in the events following those decisions – events which can be very unpleasant and distressing. The social worker may find himself (alone, or with others) compelling someone to enter a mental hospital against his will, taking away someone else's child by force, or putting another into custody. What has all this coercion to do with helping?

It is possible to devise a high-sounding intellectual answer to this question, and many books about social work contain such formulae. But when there is a confrontation full of hatred and violence which ends in the social worker using his legal powers to force someone to do what he does not want to do, these principles sound rather empty. In particular, the social worker himself is unlikely to be able to retain a firm grasp of them in the heat of battle, let alone to use them constructively. It is easy enough to recognise in tranquillity that all such situations contain a more or less serious threat to the safety and security of the person himself or of others, and that in each a law defines the acceptable limit of these threats. But in none of them is there a hard and fast definition of the law of what constitutes grounds for statutory removal or detention. So each involves the social worker in making a judgment of the seriousness of the threat, as well as in the nasty business of carrying through his decisions.

One part of the nightmare of such situations for the social worker is the complexity and intangibility of the matters to be decided. Every judgment the social worker makes involves a host of social, moral and even political dilemmas, so that any critical academic worth his salt could question each decision from half a dozen theoretical perspectives. Yet at the time, what is more likely to plague the worker is nothing so abstract as a philosophical scruple. He is usually beset by an overwhelming feeling of personal discomfort, of shame or terror or both. He is sickened by the implicit or explicit violence he is using, yet probably equally furious with the client who has provoked it, often by violence of his own. He is horribly aware both of his power and his vulnerability. He feels simultaneously an agent of brutal authority and a weak, exposed, inadequate person. These emotions can affect both what he decides to do and how he does it.

Even though every social worker must have all these conflicting feelings to some degree whenever powers of compulsion are involved, the way they are actually expressed in each worker's words and actions with the client is usually not a mixture but a polarisation at one extreme or another. What I have observed of many students doing role plays of statutory interventions confirms the evidence of reading records of some social workers in real cases, and my own experience. The artificiality of the role play merely exaggerates and caricatures the form of emotional polarisation which an extreme situation provokes. It is as if the social worker can only show the clients one part of his warring emotions, and in the process loses touch with the rest, and thus with what is really happening. Some become quite unnaturally silky and soothing. Others strive inappropriately to be bright and cheerful in the face of the most bizarre reactions from the client. Others still play down their authority to the point of denial, refusing to recognise an obligation to do something about the most blatant and disastrous catastrophe or breakdown. Yet others become flustered, hurried, inflexible and blind to all the subtleties. Some assume the mechanical approach of an impersonal investigator, going through a checklist of possible faults in the system. What all seem to find so difficult is to remain natural in the very unnatural circumstances of these crises. They cannot stay true to the many-stranded realities of the situation, or their feelings about it. In this, they lose the connection between themselves and their official roles. They cannot exercise their statutory powers in a way which also conveys a consistent, credible human being.

What appears to happen is that the moment the use of legal compulsion becomes a possibility, the social worker starts to lose some of his spontaneity, flexibility and sensitivity of touch. His dislike of the authoritarian features of his role causes him either to disguise these aspects from himself, or to overemphasise them, becoming aware of his authority at the expense of everything else. Of course the clients' reactions are likely to reinforce either of these opposites if they reject the notion that the social worker's involvement can be of any benefit to them. They will either increase his desire to be nice, kind and reasonable, however inappropriate this may be; or exaggerate his sense of his official obligations by denying their own responsibility and their need for his presence.

Thus part of the social worker's discomfort lies in the difficulty of seeing the imposition of himself and his compulsory powers on people as being consistent with his notion of himself as a helper. One reason why he can become unnaturally 'helpful' is his need to remain consistent with his stereotype of helpfulness. Alternatively he may split off such interventions from the helping part of his work, and treat them as something completely different, an unpleasant duty to be performed in quite another spirit. He cannot encompass coercion and helping in the same notion. He cannot imagine himself doing anything so nasty to those clients he helps. Still less could he think of doing such a thing to a friend or a neighbour.

Yet I myself did almost exactly that a few years ago, when I took a friend back to a mental hospital against his will – and would have arranged for him to be compulsorily admitted if he had resisted. Paul was a patient in the mental hospital (this was before I worked there), receiving treatment on a voluntary basis. The main reason he was there was a morbidly suspicious and occasionally persecutory attitude to his wife. One weekend when he was home on leave I received a terrified phone call from her. He had been brooding and mistrustful, and had been looking at her in a hateful way. Then he had suddenly grabbed her and tied her to a chair. He had told her he was going to kill her, and himself. He had taken a lot of tablets and turned his attention to her, but had collapsed before he had done her any harm. She had escaped to someone else's house, but begged me to go and see that he was safe, and to get him back to hospital.

I rang the hospital and told them what I intended doing, and then went round to his house. I was extremely frightened, not being sure which I dreaded more, to find him in a coma, or to find him alert and furious, knowing I knew where his wife was but wouldn't tell him. He answered the door looking terrible. He was pale and very tense; his face muscles were taut and his hands clenched angrily. He was about my age and build, and I was very aware of a physical threat in the air. The room was darkened, and I felt he was sizing me up. It was a few moments before he asked me to sit down. I told him I knew what had happened that afternoon. He looked at me very menacingly when I mentioned his wife. I said I was going to take him back to hospital. I made no attempt to elaborate or explain – all that seemed redundant. Very few words passed between us, but I tried to convey to him that within the terms of our friendship, I was determined to get him back straight away. He still looked bitter and full of hate, and for a moment I thought he would refuse. Then, without saying any more, he went upstairs to pack his things. I paced up and down in the living room, imagining him cutting his throat or hanging himself while I waited. Eventually he came down with his suitcase and we got in the car. All the way to the hospital I was worried that he might jump out or attack me. When we got there, he went in without a word, still looking very angry. But when I visited him a few days later he was much better. We have remained friends, and he and his wife were eventually reunited. Several years later they are living together happily again.

This incident had many of the features of a statutory

intervention, though not all. Paul was not looking for my help. He was not pleased to see me, and he did not want to go back to hospital. There was a clear threat of violence, and I was afraid. He would not have gone back of own accord, and probably if anyone else had come he would have resisted, maybe violently. But for all his hostility, Paul did not have the basic mistrust of me that stems from a fear of the unknown. In spite of his mood of murderous anger and suspicion, he was sane enough to recognise me as the friend with whom he had shared many good laughs, and who had helped him in other troubles. Equally I knew him as an intelligent and amusing companion as well as a dangerous madman. So there was a basis for some naturalness and normality between us, even though neither of us referred to it directly. I certainly did not appeal to Paul as a friend, or say anything so fatuous as, 'You know you can trust me', when it was quite plain that, at one level, he most emphatically did not.

Statutory intervention

The other important feature of this example was that I was in no doubt that Paul needed to be in hospital, and would if necessary have called the authorities to compel him. As a friend, I felt that the hospital was the right place for him to be, for his own sake, before he did something even worse. This certainty on my part probably helped both of us. If I had disbelieved or doubted his wife, I would have been cast as an investigator, trying to make an assessment of a situation, asking questions of an already overwrought man, whose anger was already near boiling point.

Yet this is precisely what the social worker often has to do. It is only rarely that he arrives to find an instantly clear-cut situation – such as a child who has been seriously injured, or so obviously neglected as to make the need for immediate removal quite plain. Even then, it is hard enough to act fairly and decisively, explaining firmly to angry or threatening parents the legal grounds for such removal, their rights and their opportunities to see the child. But at least in such circumstances the social worker's role is quite simple, very much like that of a policeman, firmly applying the law.

Far more frequently, the situation is much more ambiguous. The whole point of having social workers rather than policemen to investigate allegations about maltreatment of children is the possibility of a more flexible approach to deal with such ambiguity, by combining helpfulness with realism. Ideally, the social worker should embody some of the essential qualities of a good policeman and of a good friend, without being either. He should be able to cope with ambiguity and ambivalence, with hostility and hope. He needs to be able to respond to more than one message at once, to recognise and take account of contradictions and confusions. To arrive at the truth about a family situation he needs to be able to pick up matters of importance from hints and things that are left half-said. If he can stay calm and patient, avoid panic, look and listen, he may reach the heart of the family's relationships more quickly than by rushing to premature conclusions of his own. As I suggested in the last chapter, trying to define and limit problems is self-protective and unhelpful. People can be deterred and frustrated by naive or over-zealous attempts to tidy up what they know to be much worse messes than the social worker can bear to hear about. But they can also be discouraged by a social worker who fails to recognise glimmers of hope in an otherwise gloomy picture. Yet with all this need for sensitivity to mixed feelings and complexity, the worker still has to be able to pick up and respond quickly to well-disguised signs of real suffering, cruelty or neglect, and to act decisively to rescue the victim, whatever the quality of his previous relationship with the parents.

Here again I would suggest that much of the art of staying alive to ambiguous situations in such a way as to form sound judgments and carry them through with parents in fair and human ways lies in the social worker staying alive to all the different aspects of his own mixed feelings. To stay in touch, realistic yet sensitive, requires him to be in tune with his own head and his heart. The process needed seems to be a rigorous self-examination, often carried out during the investigatory interview itself. Am I anxious and afraid of these parents? If so, of what exactly, and of whom, and why? If not, why not?

Who or what is reassuring me, and on what basis? Am I really placing myself in the position of the child, or simply responding to the parents' needs? Very often in such an investigation there is no absolutely clear factual evidence. The social worker's assessment has to be based on whether the parents' reactions ring true, and this in turn can sometimes only be judged by the effects they produce on him. He has to try to reach a decision on whether there is a real crisis, on whether to act, and how, using many subjective clues. When he has done this, it is equally essential for him to try to explain his assessment to the parents – not necessarily in the form of a final judgment, but at least as a sharing of the impression he has got, his working hypotheses for future action. If his reactions to them have been an important factor in the formation of such a provisional assessment, he should try to communicate something about these reactions.

Sometimes this process of feeding back to parents the feelings they provoke in the social worker can be a part of the process of reaching an assessment. In the last chapter I suggested it was often the best way to initiate an adult relationship, a sharing of responsibility. But even where this is not possible – as when parents are denying glaring facts, or bristling with hostility – the worker may serve two useful purposes in telling them what he feels they are doing to him. First, he may clear his own mind, and free himself for a more balanced all-round decision. Simply by saying, 'I feel you are pushing me (intimidating me, wheedling me, tricking me, wearing me down) into doing something now which all of us may regret later because . . . ', he may break down some of the constraints on his thinking and actions which such emotional pressures impose. He may regain his own balance, and in the process also do something to create more honesty in the relationship at the time. But second, even if parents cannot use this sort of comment in that context, they may remember that it has been said, and be able to use it later.

One of the many things that can make it very difficult for a social worker to stay in touch is his reaction to violence itself, or even the threat of it. Simply seeing a fight or an injury can induce a kind of panic in some otherwise calm and perceptive workers. In training students for these interviews, we sometimes stage a fairly realistic punch-up as a way of introducing this factor. In some, it produces an over-reaction, an obsessive attention to the risk of damage through violence, at the expense of its context. This can lead to the worker becoming blind to obvious signals that the causes of violence have disappeared, and along with them the dangers of injury. But some others who are equally frightened of violence try to deny their fear and suppress the panic it induces. This can make them apparently insensitive to an atmosphere of real terror and menace. Pretending to themselves they are not afraid, they fail to pick up the hurt and fear of the victims of violence. Thus they underestimate the risks of the situation, and may leave vulnerable individuals to their fate at the hands of those who have systematically intimidated them. This seems to have been an element in at least one of the major recent child-care scandals in which a child was killed in spite of social work supervision.

Another pattern I have noticed in role plays of statutory interventions is that the social worker sometimes concentrates attention on the *less* threatening and disturbed one of a couple, on the apparent pretext that he or she is doing most of the talking. A good example of this was contained in Tony Parker's television play about a battered child, *When the Bough Breaks*. The social worker deceived herself into believing that the big, hulking, inarticulate father was the probable battering parent, and spent time with him, largely ignoring his much more broodingly silent, resentful young wife. In fact, such resentment as the man displayed was largely a protection of and distraction from the much more dangerous anger of the woman. At a more primitive emotional level, the worker had been deterred from paying any attention to the woman by her glowering looks and the feelings of rejection and resentment she put out. The man was a much safer proposition; his resistance was reasonable by comparison.

When the social worker decides to use his statutory powers to remove a child, or to admit an adult to a mental hospital, he often meets the accusation that he does not really care about the person involved, and is acting officiously, high-handedly and in an unnecessarily authoritarian manner. Sometimes, of course, the accusation is well-founded, and the worker should always take it seriously. But often it is hardest to deal with when it is least true. When the social worker cares a great deal about the person concerned, and about others in the family, he feels helplessly angry about this accusation, yet can say nothing effective to answer it. He may well have to accept angry and unfair comments at the time, and hope that his future actions will rebut them. He may also have to accept without comment criticisms coming from people who themselves have acted callously or carelessly, and who, by accusing him, are trying to assuage their own guilt.

Now that I work inside a mental hospital I am not often directly involved either in compulsory admissions or in removal of children from parents, but I do frequently work with people who have recently had such experiences with other social workers. I find that their distorted perceptions of the social workers' motives and actions are very much more readily modified if the same workers continue to visit them, and demonstrate their concern by keeping alive their own relationship and links with the family. Persistence in facing the anger of the client, in overcoming their own guilt and resentment about a painfully unpleasant process, are much more effective ways of restoring the client's realism and faith than reassuring comments at the time, followed by silence and absence. It is no easy thing for a social worker to visit someone who was violent or hateful, on a strange ward, not knowing what version the hospital staff have been given of those events, or what state of mind the client is in. But the courage required to do this is more than matched by the benefit to the client.

There are many things to deter a social worker from following up the aftermath of a statutory intervention. The sheer nastiness of the process of tearing someone away from his home and family is one factor. It is easier to try to forget about the whole series of events, and to imagine that the person himself and his family want to do the same. What this ignores is the fact that often only the social worker concerned can help them work through the sequence again and get it into perspective. Either they cannot remember the details, or they tend to distort them to justify their attitudes and actions. Another factor is the duty system, under which the social worker called out to deal with a crisis is not necessarily allocated the case afterwards. This practice often involves a collusion with the first notion, that it is in some sense better to get a new social worker, who was not involved in that sordid scene, to start afresh. Third, where someone has been admitted to an institution or some other kind of care, the social worker may feel somewhat redundant and irrelevant, or just uncomfortable about visiting. He can convince himself that the residential staff are doing all that the client requires, or that he will only unsettle him. Yet the social worker's role is often very important in preserving a sense of continuity in a client's life, in keeping alive his past, his links with family, friends and neighbours. No residential staff can grasp and retain all the elements in the client's previous circumstances, and no new home can understand all the things that were important to someone in their old home. The social worker can be of real help to the staff as well as to the client by offering a perspective for seeing him in a new setting in terms of some of the features of his previous one.

All this may be even more important where a client has been removed to a custodial establishment for breaking the law. The element of custody or punishment introduces an added unpleasantness, and the client's past misdeeds can dominate perceptions of him by others, or even his perceptions of himself. As a probation officer I regarded regular visiting of people in prison or borstal as a very vital task. It seemed important to keep alive the client's sense of himself as a worthwhile person, his consciousness of other parts of his personality than the criminal ones, and his awareness of feelings that could not be safely expressed in the institutional world. Of course it was also a way of keeping him in touch with the outside world, which otherwise seemed so remote. The longer the sentence, or the more frequent the terms of imprisonment, the more significance the visits had. Sometimes my contacts with prisoners continued over many years.

An example of one such person may serve to illustrate the

relevance of links with the past and keeping alive a network of contacts with the world outside for the sake of the future. For nearly ten years I had as one of my clients a young man who was on borstal licence (after-care supervision) when I first met him. Tony was born in the town where I worked, but his father had been a coloured serviceman. His mother had married a Birmingham man when Tony was about ten years old, and they had gone to live in the Midlands. He was soon in trouble, and sent first to approved school and then to Borstal, the latter sentence for a serious assault. On returning to the town of his birth, after wandering round the country for a time, he met and married Janet, a local girl who herself had had a difficult childhood. The marriage was stormy from the start. Tony survived his period of licence, but soon afterwards was in trouble again, and sent to prison – the start of a disastrous spell of about four years. During this sentence, Janet was often frightened and tearful, feeling inadequate and abandoned with their small child. But when he came home there were quarrels, debts, another baby on the way and soon fresh offences and a longer sentence. This time she started a pattern of promiscuity and extravagance, which was repeated during his subsequent spells of imprisonment. Rent arrears accumulated, and they were evicted from their house. Janet neglected the children when he was away, and the third child died as a small baby. The elder two were received into care. Finally, Tony was given a four-year sentence, and Janet decided to divorce him, keeping only the fourth child, and leaving the others in a children's home. Tony was sent to a long-term prison, having lost his home, his wife and his children, and with an utterly bleak future to face when he was finally released.

I visited Tony every two months throughout this sentence. At first he was full of anger and bitterness. He raged against his wife, against the prison system, against those who were caring for his children. He was aggressive and violent in the prison, and was punished. We talked about all these things, and then looked at the pattern of his life, and he was eventually able to tell me a great deal about his childhood. He had been unable to get on with his mother and stepfather, and had been first in care for a time and then sent to approved school for a trivial offence. The fact that his own children were in care hurt and saddened him terribly, because he had felt so abandoned. He was also reminded of his approved school experience because now, as then, he knew he would not go out to his family and home. He remembered being bullied and humiliated, and how this had been the start of his long history of violence. Gradually Tony's anger drained away, and as he took stock of his situation his despair became even stronger. He felt he was growing older, that life was passing him by. He was losing his good looks and his great physical strength, wasting himself in a round of trivial tasks. He began to worry that his hair was starting to fall out. He had doubts about who he was, and felt he was becoming just a prisoner. He had nowhere to go when he left prison. He wondered whether he should go to a city and try to pass for a West Indian – but he had no knowledge at all of their culture, and felt from what experience he had had of them that they would reject him. By this time I was his only visitor; he had lost all his other links with the world outside.

I felt that Tony had held on to his humanity and to the core of his identity through this sentence, but that he desperately needed some roots, and the sense that there was somewhere he still belonged. I doubted whether his old friends had really forgotten him or written him off. I knew them all, because they had all been in trouble, but by now they had all been straight for several years, and were married and had families of their own. The first one I went to see was delighted to hear of Tony again, and started to write to him and visit him. I then found another ex-offender of about his age, whom he did not know, but who was an equally aggressive person, and was willing to give him lodgings – who else would have had Tony in their house? Finally, I did a tour of all his old comrades, and arranged for them all to be in a pub in the centre of town at midday on the day he was discharged from prison. I met him at the bus station and took him to the labour exchange and the social security. We got his money just in time to reach the pub by noon. Tony was overwhelmed by the welcome back he received, but in a couple of hours it was as if he had never been away. I never had another official contact with him again. I met him in the street a few times and offered to see him at the office, but he assured me that he had no need of my help (he had always kept closely in touch before.) Two years later I received a Christmas card, telling me that he was now remarried and had a child. I visited him in his flat in a nearby town. He was proud of his achievements in staying out of trouble and making a new start. A lot of the old tension and anger were gone. Tony had reverted to his mother's surname, but was still in touch with his old friends.

In this example, I felt that both sides of my work with Tony were equally important. I went on visiting him while he reached his lowest ebb, when he was almost drowning in his own hatred and despair. After blaming me and everybody else for his fall into this pit, he was gradually able to see how he constantly re-enacted his early rejection and punishment. He had tried to demand and wrest from Janet and others the love and security he needed, to punch and kick his way out of the trap of humiliation and degradation that surrounded him. But even when he faced the worst about himself and where he was, Tony was in no position to do anything about it. He needed other people, and I was his only connection with the world outside. If I had not been in a position to rally his friends, he might have remained a needy client for many years. As it was, he ceased at once to have any need for me at all.

Supervision

So far I have mainly discussed statutory work in which the social worker's investigation leads to the removal or detention of an individual member of a family. I want to turn now to the more common outcome of such interventions – supervision, either on a voluntary basis or as a result of a court order. In a sense, supervision begins from the moment the social worker starts his contact with a client who has not asked for help. The assessment is in itself supervisory, and sets the tone of any further dealings between the worker and the family. The social worker's presence is by virtue of his statutory authority, and rests at least partly on his powers to do something more drastic, such as take a child away, or recommend to a court that a delinquent should be in care or custody.

Yet the basis for supervision is quite different from that of removal or detention. The social worker's job is to try to help the client hold on to a difficult situation, until the risk (to the child) or the threat (of delinquency) is reckoned to have passed. This is not at all the same as compelling him to go somewhere he does not want to go, because that compulsion rests on the assumption that he *cannot* hold on to the situation, and that it is likely to break down, with a danger of further injuries or offences.

In probation, of course, the distinction between the two kinds of authority is clear cut. If the offender is placed on probation then the probation officer supervises him and tries to hold him to the task of staying out of trouble, however difficult this may be. But if he re-offends seriously, then it is part of the probation officer's job to indicate to the court what went wrong during supervision, and if no other alternative is available, to recommend imprisonment. But in social services work the distinctions between supervision, care and custody are all more blurred, and this makes it the more important for a social worker to define the scope and purposes of his powers to the family. Otherwise, in his desire to be helpful, he may obscure the pitfalls of an unsignposted path that can lead the unsuspecting from one to the next and end up in the third.

Using the supervision of parents alleged to have maltreated their young children as the example, it seems worth considering some of the things that are likely to make the social worker's continued presence bearable and constructive for those receiving his visits. The first notion I would suggest is that the parents should be quite clear about the reason why the social worker is coming, what is alleged, and what he can do about it. They need to know that the social worker has a statutory power to remove children under certain circumstances, and roughly what these circumstances are. They need to know that if a child is being badly neglected or ill-treated, the social worker will not only be empowered to act, but obliged to act. They need to have some idea of what is being expected of them as parents, and also what rights they have against undue interference or unjustified removal of the child – for instance, their rights of appeal against any decision. Without listing these things parrot-fashion, the social worker should try to make them clear.

The second notion, which is in tension with the first, is that parents should be encouraged to feel that they can share negative feelings and impulses and the worst aspects of their family circumstances with the social worker within an atmosphere of goodwill and genuine concern. There is little value in supervision which takes the form of exhortations to parents to be braver or stronger or more virtuous. When the social worker has not listened to parents' rejecting and destructive emotions, their fears of inadequacy and failure, such demands provoke anger and frustration. Equally, the parents are unlikely to be honest and open if they suspect that confessions of violent thoughts, words or actions will automatically be used as evidence of their unsuitability to bring up their child. Similarly, they should feel that they can be critical, angry or hostile to the worker without losing his goodwill. It is difficult to reconcile these ideas with the notion of clarity about legal functions, but without them there is little opportunity for helping. I have suggested throughout that people in real trouble can best be helped by sharing what is worst for them, and in these situations it is nearly always some very strongly destructive feelings or fantasies. Somehow the worker must find a balance between his determination to discover the truth for the child's sake, and his willingness, if he hopes to establish a relationship of trust and sharing with the parents, to recognise both positives and negatives in the care they provide. He has to find a way of being open to the parents' weaknesses which offers them all-round understanding, but he must never cease to consider the plight of the child.

The third notion is that the social worker ought to try to establish a relationship with the child or children. Since it is always the child's interests which are the paramount purpose of his intervention, he should always be trying to place himself imaginatively in the child's situation, to form some picture of what the child's life must be like. Even if the child is too young to speak to him, he should at least spend some time with him, if possible in such a way as to avoid making the parents anxious and hostile. If he comes to suspect that the parents are not being frank, are evading issues or concealing facts, he owes it to the child to be dogged and determined in confronting them with his suspicions, even at the risk of being wrong. His authority in such situations derives from the child's vulnerability and helplessness more than from his agency's statutory powers. However, he must also be willing for his hunches or intuitions about a child's safety to be falsified, to give parents the chance to show him that he has been wrong.

It is often hardest to keep the balance between these aspects of supervision in a case involving alleged maltreatment of children when the parents themselves have had deprived backgrounds, and live turbulent, quarrelsome lives. One reason is that such parents often need help with many other problems, and are therefore long-term clients of social services departments. This means that there are always other issues than the several just mentioned which arise in supervision. Another is that their standards of care of their children are often very variable. When they are getting on well together, the children are quite well looked after. When they fall out, or one of them has a change of mood, the care deteriorates dramatically. Such families tend to lead lives which are punctuated by crises and disasters. The social worker has to find a way of helping with these within the context of a long-term relationship of honesty and good faith.

This was something I found very difficult as a young probation officer. Even though I had no statutory responsibility for child care, I had under my supervision several young men with deprived backgrounds, who had been in institutions for adolescent delinquency, who were now married with young children. My difficulty was not in establishing an initial relationship of trust. I seemed able in early interviews with both my client and his wife to be recognised as someone willing to help them with the aspects of their lives they found most problematic – emotional closeness, feelings of mutual dependence, love and trust, and providing the same for their children. They quickly accepted me, welcomed me, seemed to see me as someone special. Yet the very qualities they most valued

– my empathy and liking for them – were in the longer term a kind of weakness in our relationships. For in accepting me as a 'good' person, they seemed to endow me with all the qualities they could not consistently achieve. I came to embody and personify the feelings which they found hardest to express to each other or their children. Instead of experiencing and developing their own strengths, and helping each other, they saw me as being their strength and their help. And so, after a short honeymoon when everything changed for the better, they started to get worse again, to revert to their old pattern, sometimes in an even more chaotic and unacceptable form. I had become their ideal self, while they had become caricatures of their bad selves. The more this happened, the more they insisted that they needed me, that they could not manage without me. They regarded me as more to them than a social worker, they regarded me as one of the family. In a sense I had become 'the family' itself, while they had become the disruptive agents of the family's destruction.

I had plenty of clues that this was happening, but I also had strong reasons for ignoring them. In some ways the role was a very rewarding one. I was loved and I was needed, and however ghastly the crises were, I was always trusted and turned to by all concerned. Even when they were shouting and swearing and hurting each other, they treated me with a special kind of gentleness and politeness, giving me endless cups of incredibly bad tea, and asking solicitously about my health. They were people not much younger than myself, who had children much the same age as mine, and with whom I found it easy to identify. I liked them, and saw goodness and potential as well as difficulties and destructiveness. I refused to recognise how they used me to damage each other and themselves. Because I was near them in age, I could not see how much they treated me as an idealised parent. I really only finally accepted this when one couple told me, with delight, that they had had a Christmas card from his long-lost father. To my amazement, they produced their card from me. They had somehow contrived to read my signature as 'Your dad'.

One good example of this process was my relationship

with Tony and Janet, whom I mentioned earlier in this chapter. They had both been rejected by their parents, and were disliked and distrusted by most older people, officials and authority figures. Tony was scowling, quick-tempered and demanding, and he could be a bully. Janet was flirtatious, frivolous and unreliable. He never kept a job for long; she was a bad manager and a slovenly housewife. Yet from the first there was a genuine liking and trust between us. Tony found that he could not intimidate or fool me. I could tell when he was shooting a line, and could very directly tell him to 'Come off it'. He would rather enjoy this, and break into a broad smile of genuine amusement, when if someone else had said the same thing he would probably have hit them. One time, when he had just come out of prison, and was trying to get himself and Janet re-established (with immense amounts of practical help from me) he came bursting into the office, took the stairs in about three strides, crashed through my door, and hurled himself at my desk, bringing his fist down on it and demanding more help. I told him very firmly to shut the door and sit down, which he did; but he went on shouting at me, accusing me of never having helped him the way probation officers were supposed to help. I hadn't got him a job or a flat, and now he had no decent clothes, and it was about time I gave him some money to buy some. He knew very well that the probation service had a special fund, a box, to help people like him. At this I retorted, with real anger, 'Look here Tony, I am not a box, I am a person, and a person that's put up with you for several years, so stop talking to me as a box, and start talking to me as a person'. At this he stopped shouting, smiled, relaxed, sat back, and became quite human and reasonable.

Yet in spite of these advantageous conditions for honesty and directness in our relationship, I was unhelpful to Tony and Janet because I could not resist the long-term role of idealised parent. I was too available and willing to respond to every crisis. My offer of myself was total, without the anchor of my own identity and needs. It had no proper shape or boundaries. It was as if I was a kind of inflatable helper whom they could blow up to enormous proportions, and who took the shape their fantasies decreed – usually of 'superparent'. Ultimately I was so reliable, persistent and genuinely forgiving that they could invest all their best features in me, and be as bad as or worse than before. Thus even though in interviews with them I would try to be honest, to share their pain, to hold them to their obligations to each other and the children, ultimately my relationship with them was unhelpfully collusive, because there was a hidden agenda. Each side had an investment in the other, whatever they did, however badly they behaved. They needed me, and I needed to be needed by them, and all of us knew this at some level. This was why Tony could afford not to get angry when I challenged him. It was only towards the end of my contact with him that I was able to get him to be really angry with me, by challenging him in a way that showed I meant to call him to account for his actions.

The results of that collusion were destructive. After the first phase, Tony re-offended regularly, and their marriage and care of the children deteriorated. By the time the third child was born, Janet herself was on probation to a colleague, and the children's department were also involved. The baby's death was not caused by neglect, but he and the other two children had been very poorly cared for immediately before his death. She was convicted of neglecting them, and they were taken into care. I had been seeing her during this period, and I felt I was more responsible for failing to do something about this series of disasters than the others who were visiting her. I was in a better position to help than they were, but something of the falseness of my role prevented me from doing so. Neither Tony nor Janet nor myself could ever really forgive ourselves or each other for our failures during those events. In the end, Tony and Janet were bad for each other, and I was bad for them both. My final visits to them, in their squalid flat, were the uncomfortable and slightly hollow legacy of what had come to be a sham. We were all disillusioned by then. We had come to realise that for five years we had created and pretended to believe in a myth about their relationship and my power to help them which could not be sustained.

In such long-term relationships with very deprived and destructive people, the social worker needs to strive to be ordinary if he is to be helpful. He must expect to have strong feelings of attachment to and affection for his clients, and for there to be mutual ties of love and loyalty, which contain elements of idealisation. But he must resist the temptation to be special, to have magical powers, to make everything right. He must be alive to the signals that they are seeing him as specially understanding and helpful, and that he is becoming quite abnormally tolerant and kind, available and self-sacrificing. In the long run, such people can benefit much more from a social worker who stays a real, flesh-and-blood person, with his own needs and foibles, his off-days and bad moods, who asserts these, displays them, shares them and is not ashamed of them. Even though in the short run he is bound to be invaded by their fears and fantasies, pervaded by their strong and primitive feelings, he must in the longer term retain his grip on his own reality.

Case Example

The example I have just given represents one possible way in which long-term statutory work with familes can go wrong. A social worker can become so taken up in the role of guardian and protector of young, deprived parents as to be blind to obvious indications that their care of their children has become unacceptable. In tragic cases of cruelty and neglect, there have been indications that the social workers felt they had specially 'good relationships' with parents, which made them unwilling to be associated with certain unpleasantly authoritative tasks. Because of this special quality of their relationships social workers refused to listen to allegations from neighbours or act upon them. Even where parents themselves hinted at violence, or drew attention to it, they seemed unable to recognise the evidence of their eyes and ears.

But there are quite different ways in which social workers can act unhelpfully in such cases. The following rather lengthy example is an account written by a parent whom I shall call Mrs Miller of her dealings with social services department over her daughter Shirley. Earlier in this chapter, I suggested that social workers should try to ensure that parents know the purposes of their visits, and their legal powers; that parents feel able to trust in the goodwill of social workers and confident in confessing faults and failures; and that social workers should pay attention to the feelings of the children themselves. Mrs Miller felt that none of these things were done in her daughter's case.

Mrs Susan Miller and her husband Michael were both in their mid-thirties; their two children, Peter and Shirley, were then aged six and five. Mr Miller was self-employed, and earned a good income by working long hours. The family owned their own terrace house, which was furnished and equipped to a high standard. They were on the telephone, owned a car and a boat. They were an ordinary, successful working-class family. Shirley was a hole-in-the-heart baby, but grew into a very lively and energetic toddler – indeed she was more active and exhausting than the average child. She was boisterous, adventurous and rather accident-prone. She demanded a good deal of her mother's energy and attention. The following is Mrs Miller's written account of the events before and after the intervention of the social services department.

> Fifteen months prior to Shirley starting school, I had been suffering from nervous exhaustion. I became so weak that the lightest task was hard work. I was 35 years old, and what with helping my husband with his business, keeping the house and children clean, I became very low at times. I called my doctor, who gave me librium tablets, but what I needed was a good rest, which was impossible. When Peter started school two months after I was ill, I slowly picked up. When Shirley went afternoons it helped a lot more. The twelve months before Peter went to school he was more active than Shirley.
>
> At the end of March, Shirley went to school three Thursday afternoons. The first time, she used to want 'to do her own thing'. She couldn't keep still, and just wasn't ready to conform. She was good the second week. The third Thursday she used to want to play in the playhouse and not go in the classroom.

It was decided to put her in the special unit which has only about fifteen children and three teachers. Mrs Griffiths managed Shirley very well and found she did respond to firm consistent handling. She found Shirley needed a lot of attention and was very affectionate. Shirley liked her very much.

In this special unit there were some handicapped children and some with speech problems, and some were a bit backward. Shirley didn't talk about any friends she had made in this class, but she was popular in the playground and made a couple of friends in the dinner hour (I used to take her down to school by 1 o'clock).

She saw the Educational Psychologist, Mrs Lever, who didn't think she would be in the special unit very long. I told Mrs Griffiths that Shirley took a lot out of me, and with her brother, who was only a year older, very hard work. Shirley was a little slow growing up, and full of mischief and hyper-active. She was a real 'bright spark', very sharp, but needed a lot of love and attention. She asked me if I would like some help with her, and I said yes. I told her my husband worked virtually seven days a week and couldn't give me any help.

About the second week of the six week summer holiday, a Health Visitor, Mrs Johnson and another lady came to take Shirley to Broadmead playgroup. [This was some 15 miles away, though the Millers lived in a city.] Shirley enjoyed herself, but came home very tired, but more full of energy than ever, and wouldn't go to sleep till about 9.30 p.m. On the third day she broke her arm. It was an accident, *but* Shirley needs a lot of supervision as she sees no fear, and tries to do more than she is capable of. She stayed at home for about ten days and with her broken arm she was worse than ever, because she was still trying to do the same things. She just couldn't slow down, I had to watch her like a hawk in case she broke something else. Mrs Johnson visited and saw what she was like.

[It subsequently emerged that the other lady was from the social services department, who provided transport to the playgroup. After Shirley broke her arm, they did not visit the

Millers at any stage to express concern or inquire after her recovery.]

> She then went to Blackthorn [15 miles away in the opposite direction] daily for a week, and then home for a week. During that week she became the worst she had ever been. I used to take her down to the park nearly all day, and she constantly fell on her broken arm and we had many a battle because she wouldn't hold my hand, walking along. I had a temper tantrum over the shop, she sat on the floor and swore at me, because I wouldn't let her have another packet of crisps, and she wouldn't hold my hand crossing the road on the way back. I got her home, I didn't smack her, I shook her up against the cupboard door, and said, 'You *will* hold my hand when I say so and you can spit and swear so much as you like, but you won't get away with it.' Two days later I had a minor repeat of that incident, I was in tears when I got home, and I shouted at her, and she started to cry. Mr Field [a social worker] then came to the house and I told him how I had shook her. He took Shirley to Bellcoombe playgroup on the Thursday, she came home swinging on his arms and legs knowing that he was soft. Michael would soon tell her to cut out the nonsense, and she would behave herself, she never played Michael up very often.
>
> Mrs Miller underlined the next paragraph of her account.
>
> *If I have painted Shirley as a little horror, it is because she was never anything like as bad before the summer holidays, and the playschools with all the different supervisors and not much discipline. She was also under physical strain with her broken arm. This wasn't a good basis for her to start school all day.*

In conversation, Mr Miller emphasised that he and his wife welcomed the arrival of the social workers – both the one that took Shirley to the first playgroup, and the second worker, Mr Field, who came following the incident when Mrs Miller had shaken Shirley. He said he felt at last they were getting some help with Shirley, which they had needed for a long time. They wanted to confide in the social worker because they felt bad about what had happened, and felt they should be able to handle Shirley better.

Mrs Miller's account continues,

> After about 10 days at school, [Shirley started school full time that September] I told Mrs Winter (her new teacher) that Shirley was a different child. She was good after school and I could cope with her at weekends. I asked nearly every day how she was, I was told, quite good, not so good, and some days good. This was the *only* contact I had with the school in the three weeks. I never spoke to her headmaster, Mr Havelock.
>
> On the Wednesday of the third week, I was told by Mr Havelock outside school very casually that Shirley has to see the doctor 2.15 on Friday, ask your husband to come. I said, 'If he is working he can't, if he isn't working I will ask him.' That was the exact words and *all* that was said.
>
> I told Michael, he said, 'Shirley is always seeing doctors (she has a hole in the heart). I don't need to go with you when she sees a doctor.' On the Friday I left at 2 p.m. to go to the school. Just after I left Mr Field called for Michael who was on the garage roof mending a leak. Mr Field told him Shirley was stopping the other children from learning. They had already had one meeting about her. But this was the first time either of us were told.
>
> I knew she wasn't really ready for school (though half-way through the previous term I thought she was). But I had no idea they couldn't cope with her.
>
> I was there at 2.15 prompt. I thought it was the medical all children have when they first start school. Shirley had already been examined. I talked to Dr Brown [a child psychiatrist] and told him that I had gone down in the holidays and I needed forty winks in the day, and that two children were sometimes too much for me and that sometimes I wished I hadn't had a second child, and Michael didn't understand why I used to get so tired.

Mrs Miller underlined the next paragraph.

This was interpreted in Court by Dr Brown as he felt I had a total rejection of the child and she wasn't loved and that was why she had behaviour problems.

This is not so, Shirley was a planned baby. (My own doctor will verify this.) She had to share our time and affection with her brother, but Daddy has made more fuss of her and cuddled her more than her brother. I told Dr. Brown that when Shirley was good she was an absolute darling, and had a strong personality.

Mr Field the social worker came in, I was very surprised to see him, I thought, 'What is he doing here?' Then the headmaster Mr Havelock came in. Shirley had already been examined, she had a bruise the size of an apple on her thigh, which hurt her. She had done this falling off the climbing frame at school (when she still had her arm in a short plaster). This was verified by Mr Havelock. But a fuss was made of it. I said, 'Surely you don't think I did it?' They said she had a bruise an inch long near the big bruise, which Shirley told them Daddy had smacked her the night before with a stick. I said, 'Yes he did'. I told them, Shirley and her brother were fighting and rolling on the floor getting proper silly. I told them repeatedly to stop but they took no notice. The boy then stopped, and sat down to watch t.v., but Shirley kept on. We don't smack the children with our hands if they are naughty, we have a thin stick and smack them on the leg. Daddy smacked her on the leg once, she didn't cry, but she sat still for an hour and a half and watched t.v. I bathed her in the sink that morning and I only saw the big bruise.

The thing is that Shirley has always got bruises on her, because she knocks herself and doesn't cry, so you don't know how she got a particular bruise. Mr Field said she was always covered in bruises. Mr Havelock must have told them this, but he himself said to me at a later date that she was accident prone and always falling down.

Another incident was either discussed then or at a later meeting, but it was brought up as 'the new evidence brought to light'. Shirley was mucking about while dressing for school, and wouldn't let me put her sandals on. I gave her a little smack on the leg with her sandal. She didn't want to go to school that morning and already had a little cry, and I told her she had to go to school. This new term she wasn't so eager to go to school. She cried in the playground and she told Mr Havelock that Mummy had smacked her with her shoe. She had a fresh bruise on her knee and it was surmised that I had done it. In court Mr Field just said I had hit her with a shoe.

They decided she should go to an assessment centre. Mr Havelock said he had tried to get her into the Sheridan Clinic [a children's psychiatric unit] but she was too young. *We weren't asked if we wanted her to go to the Sheridan Clinic.* I think that it is downright bureaucracy to even mention such a thing without first asking parents. Mrs Griffiths (her first teacher) hasn't been asked to any of the meetings on Shirley.

I agree she needed experienced handling and I said I used to worry about her always falling down. I was told she would be away for a month. I agreed, but I had no choice. Mr Field left at 3 p.m. I waited till 3.30 p.m. and picked up both children from school. I arrived home about 3.45 p.m. Mr Field was filling out a form with Michael. Michael told Mr Field he didn't want Shirley away from home. He had been put away as a child and he could never understand why his mother had him put away, and he never forgot it. But he said he would sign for my sake.

We were told it was for a month. We weren't told anything about the place except it was an assessment centre. We weren't told we couldn't take her for a ride on visiting days. He said, 'I will phone you the visiting hours'. I packed up a few of her clothes and she was gone by 4 p.m. Shirley had had no tea and could have been at Meadowlands (the assessment centre) for about three hours and then in bed. Mr Field phoned later and said visting was 2-4 p.m. on Saturdays.

When Michael signed the form he asked, 'When is she going?' Mr Field said 'Now'. Michael said, 'What, right now?' We were absolutely shocked and flabbergasted.

Mr and Mrs Miller visited Meadowlands the following day, and found it more institutional than they had expected.

They met only one junior member of staff.

> When we were leaving Shirley cried and shouted after us. We were told they were used to this, she'd be all right. So we left none the wiser. I phoned every other day, but I didn't get any information. All I was told was 'Oh yes, she's all right'.
>
> On the third day after Shirley had gone, Michael began to feel very angry at the way he had been conned into it, and I was missing Shirley very much. He relived how he felt when he was put away, and he could hardly sleep at all for three nights following. He was waking up in the night shouting at me, 'I want that girl home'. He was on at me continuously, 'Why did you let her go away'. I said, 'I had no choice'. He said, 'They'll destroy her mind'.
>
> I phoned Mr Field several times and told him Michael's feelings. He came to the house one afternoon because we were going to take her away. He said, 'You can't, she is supposed to stay the month, and the school won't have her back, then what will you do?' We argued for two hours. We were on and on about how young Shirley was, how much a baby in some ways she was, and surely she could be helped without taking her away from home.

By the third week, Mr and Mrs Miller were becoming more anxious and angry. Shirley was showing more distress on their Saturday visits, crying, clinging and asking to come home. They saw no members of staff on the third Saturday.

> By the Thursday of the third week I was getting angry and I went out to bring her home. I told a lady I had come to take Shirley home. . . . They wouldn't let me see her until I saw Mr Field. I was very angry and upset. I realised my husband was right all along. I waited for two hours for Mr Field. I talked and talked to Mr Field. He said, 'I thought I talked your husband into leaving her here'.
>
> I said, 'Never will he agree'. He asked me what Michael thought of him. I said he thinks you so-called do-gooders who haven't any children of your own don't do any good at all. I told him Michael wasn't sleeping and was making

himself ill. He said, 'Tell him to go and see the doctor.' I left at 3.30, still not seeing Shirley, and I was late for meeting Peter from school.

The Millers decided that when they visited on the next Saturday (just under a week before the end of the agreed month) they would insist on taking Shirley home if she was still upset. In fact, she was asking to come home from the minute they arrived, and screamed when her mother went out of the room.

That made Michael's mind up. He told the girl we were taking her home. She said, 'I shall have to tell the social worker'. Michael said, 'You tell him, if he comes to my door I'll thump him'.

Mr Wilson, Mr Field's senior, came on Saturday evening. He saw the children. We had a long talk. Michael told him he would help me a lot more with the children. He told us later he was happy with the home situation or he would have taken her on the Saturday.

The four days we had Shirley she clung to me. She'd scream if I left the room. She wouldn't leave the room on her own. I had her two best friends in to play but she only wanted to play with her brother. She was saying, 'I like you, I love you', all the time. We promised her faithfully we would never let her go back to Meadowlands. When she went to bed, I left her door wide open (she used to want it shut before) and I had to give her a running commentary. She would ask, 'What are you doing? Where are you going?' I would say, 'I'm saying goodnight to Peter.' 'I'm going down to make a cup of tea'. She would then say, 'Which room are you going to be in?' and I would tell her, first the kitchen and then the front room. After two days of this Michael and I agreed we had done the right thing by bringing her home.

At 7.15 p.m. on Tuesday evening Mr Field and four policemen came to the door. He told us that a court order (place of safety order) had been issued on the 'light of new evidence'. My husband told Mr Field this would cost him his job, and that he was a boy doing a man's work. He said,

'Over my dead body will Shirley leave this house'. He wouldn't tell us the new evidence, we weren't given a court order. The policeman told Mr Field to go outside. I tried to explain the terrible emotional state Shirley was in. The shouting went on for one hour. Shirley woke up crying, Michael brought her down. She said, 'I don't want to go back to Meadowlands, I like you, I love you'. The policeman was able to calm Michael down once Mr Field was outside. He told Michael if he got violent it would go against him where Shirley was concerned. I went back in the police car to Meadowlands. Shirley was crying and saying, 'You come with me', all the time. When Mr Field took her I shouted, 'Mind you look after her'. *I found eleven bruises on her, the second week at Meadowlands.* She had a four inch long, inch wide, bruise in her groin. It makes me wild, no one questions a bruise unless there's a chance they can pin the bruise on us. Otherwise they couldn't care, whatever she broke.

I told the policeman and policewoman how we hadn't met the person that supervised Meadowlands or been told anything about the place, and that we could only visit on Saturdays. I was telling him this on the way there. When we arrived he said, 'Ask when you can see her'. I was told, 'On Saturday'.

I went to see Mr Wilson [senior social worker] the next day. He said, 'I can't tell you who said or what the new evidence was'. Mr Wilson asked me about the stick mark. I said, 'Yes', but I didn't realise until later that he had only just known about it, and that Mr Field was saying he didn't know about it before either. Either Mr Havelock or Dr Brown must have brought it up at the meeting they had on Tuesday.

I phoned Mrs Johnson [the Health Visitor] who was at the meeting all the time. She said there was no new evidence. They put the stick mark and the shaking together. Mr Havelock said he wouldn't have her back at school, and I think Meadowlands said they needed longer. They put this together and their seniors issued a court order. They dug up every little thing they could find to justify their actions.

When I was in the office with Mr Field and Mr Wilson, I said the court order was issued because we took Shirley away a week before her time. They said no, they would have issued it whether they had known this new evidence a month ago, or a month later. But they did know. The point of it is it wasn't new evidence, it was what we had told them. The only thing that was new was the smack on the leg with the sandal, which Mr Havelock brought up.

Mr Wilson came round that evening and denied emphatically that Mr Field knew of the stick mark before the meeting. I said, 'I'll phone Mr Havelock'. He said, 'There's no need', but Mr Havelock was away. Michael spoke to Mr Havelock on the phone a few days later. He said of course Mr Field knew about the stick mark. Michael told him of the underhand way Shirley was sent to Meadowlands and how he hadn't been told that the meeting at school was to discuss sending Shirley away, and it wasn't just to see the doctor. Mr Havelock said, 'Meadowlands developed from the meeting, it wasn't planned before'. That isn't true, something was in mind, because firstly, why ask the father to come to school in the middle of the afternoon (how could he anyway if he was working). . . . Secondly Mr Havelock said, 'I've already tried to get her into the Sheridan Clinic, but she's too young.' He told Michael that Shirley was the worst child he had ever met in his 20 years of teaching. We can't accept that. We say they have to paint her blacker than what she is to justify their underhand actions. I have asked (the staff at Meadowlands) if they thought Shirley was that bad. They couldn't accept it either. Uncle John [a housefather] told me on the phone that she had a strong personality. She used to try it on, but she could be made to do as she was told, and never bore a grudge, and she had more 'guts' than a lot of the big boys there. He also said she saw no fear. [She was by some years the youngest child at Meadowlands.] He seemed genuinely fond of Shirley.

I spoke on the phone to Mr Crosby [the Superintendent of the assessment centre] for the first time. I said, 'Why haven't we met you?' He said, 'Didn't Mr Field give you the letter I gave him?' I said, 'What letter?' He said, 'It stated the visiting hours, Thursdays and Saturdays.' I said, 'Thursdays! That's the first we've heard of that!' He said, 'It also stated that I would be available to meet you and discuss Shirley'. I said, 'We never had no letter, and that's why we were so angry, because we felt shut out from Meadowlands'.

Mr Havelock came around after that phone call, having just visited Shirley and Mr Crosby. . . . He said Shirley was constantly sucking her thumb. (Shirley *has never* sucked her thumb.) He said he thought her case was mishandled and had snowballed. It was never meant to go so far. 'This happened because you took her away.' After he left, Michael said, 'I don't like that man. He couldn't look me in the face. He's two faced. I have the feeling he's behind all this.'

We didn't visit Shirley during this fortnight. Because Michael was so angry, if he had visited her and she had cried to come home, he would have been unable to refuse, and it was distressing to Shirley to tear her apart so.

When we went to court, Shirley was outside in Mr Field's car with another social worker. She looked ill. She was very pale, she had a big cold sore on her mouth, she was clutching an envelope with some family photographs I had sent her. She started crying and asking to come home when she saw us. We couldn't stop long as we had to be in court. When we got into the waiting room we shouted, I mean shouted, and swore at Mr Wilson, about the state of Shirley outside in the car. Dr Brown and Mr Havelock didn't know that Shirley was outside till I told them. Later they both went down to see her. Mr Havelock said she looked bad. Dr Brown said she had a heavy cold. We spoke to Dr Brown and Mr Havelock and said we thought the treatment was too harsh for Shirley and I said mornings only at school would be enough. He said, 'That's an idea.'

Their solicitor read out nearly all his evidence even though the court told him not to. He said Daddy smacked her with the stick because she broke some crockery, I hit her with a shoe, and that we left Meadowlands after a visit, promising to bring her back some sweets, and she was very distressed, because we never came back. It was books we promised her, and we came right home and fetched them and her big teddy, and handed them in at the door to Miss Clarke. He asked the court for 28 days to interview two witnesses. He was given 14 days. All I managed to say was I felt the court order was issued because we took Shirley away, and how the S.S. use your voluntary evidence against you. We also asked for Shirley to be examined by a doctor. I felt so angry because we haven't been against help from people for Shirley. But we don't like being told we have no say in anything. Their attitude was, 'We do as we like. There is no compromise.' The more we spoke against their methods, the more the whole department came down on us.

We went to see Mr Crosby for the first time. He told us he did a lot of his liaison with parents through the social worker, as he doesn't push himself on parents, as some don't want to meet him. He gave us the letter we should have had five weeks before. He said, 'I hope this doesn't put you off seeking help.' He said he was given the impression, somewhere along the line, that *Shirley was backward but he certainly didn't think so*. At Meadowlands they thought she was intelligent. He also said he had met far worse children than Shirley. He also said he had not seen Mr Field to talk to. He agreed there was a lack of communication between the S.S. and Meadowlands.

We phoned Mrs Dickinson [area manager] and Mr Pollock [district manager] and said we wanted to complain about the way Mr Field had conducted the case. We said, 'As you took Shirley on a so called "safety order", because in your opinion she was at risk, why leave the other child who is only one year older?' We also said, 'The way you take one child away from a family, the stress you put them under, and if one was that way inclined, you could, and most probably did in some cases, put the child that was left behind at risk.' We said this very nastily.

The next day we had a supervision order for Peter (not by registered post). It said if they got care of Shirley they would apply for supervision for Peter. We saw Mr Wilson after. He said it would be a good thing for the department when this case was over. He apologised for the way Shirley was taken to Meadowlands. He said if he had been on the case, he would have taken us there.

We saw Mrs Dickinson and Mr Pollock. She said, 'I hear you, but I won't accept any complaints about my very experienced social worker Mr Field.' Michael said, 'You don't call two years very experienced? He is a boy doing a man's work.' She advised us to have a solicitor. Michael replied, 'You fight us on taxpayers' money, I have to work for mine. Financial difficulties add more stress. Since your department interfered you put more stress on us.' We argued for a long time. We told her of Shirley's distress on our visits. She said, 'Part of your duty as parents is to leave as painlessly as possible, and not take too much notice of a few tears.'

After we left we began to think this is their standard practice, and how can you complain about the S.S. to another member of the S.S.

We saw Mr Wilson on one or two occasions. He had changed his attitude. We had the feeling he had been told, 'Don't give at all.' He also said on one visit, 'Your wife is up in the air and you're quiet. The next time it is the other way around.' We said, 'What do you expect? We're awake half the night, seething with anger and frustration, and wishing Shirley were home.'

We visited Shirley on Thursdays and Saturdays. On three of these visits she cried for an hour and a half, not noisy crying, just genuine tears streaming down her face. I used to ask her who she liked at Meadowlands and who her friends were. She kept saying, 'I want you, I want you.' . . .

24th November: At the next court [full hearing of proceedings for a care order] Dr Brown spoke first. He mentioned the big bruise and the stick mark, and said he pressed it to see if it was a fracture and Shirley winced. The solicitor questioned him about me, and he said I was smoking a lot at the meeting and that I told him I needed a sleep in the day and that I wished I never had Shirley. The clerk of the court asked him if the playschools could have upset Shirley. He gave a non-commital answer. He said Michael should have come to the meeting. He said, 'If I had known it was to discuss a home I would have come.'

Mr Havelock was next. He said Shirley was a very disturbed child. She used to wander off lost in a little world of her own. (She used to go in the playhouse at school and play by herself.) I said to the court, Shirley has always had her brother to play with, she wasn't craving for other children's company. Sometimes she used to really enjoy playing by herself. But she was never shy with strangers. I reminded him of the time he had said when Shirley was good she was nicer than the average child and at times what an absolute darling she could be. He replied, most vehemently, 'Oh, No, I never did.' After that reply I thought 'You'll get no good from him'. (A day later we went down to school and really went for him. Michael told him, 'You took all my rights as a father away.' The argument got very stormy . . .)

Mrs Humphreys, the Meadowlands psychologist, was next. She said she had met Shirley three days after admission to Meadowlands. She said Shirley was uncooperative, couldn't be persuaded and was mucking about all the time. She met her a month later and was able to do some work with her. She was a much improved child. We asked her how two children who had been brought up the same could be so different. We said Shirley was born the way she was, you wouldn't change her, but when she was a bit older and could go out and play down the park and do more things she would be all right.

Then Mr Field was questioned. He wasn't too bad. Then the clerk of the court questioned his experience of this sort of case where the parents are *fighting* for the child. He said he had been on a couple of cases. He said he never received the letter from Mr Crosby and that he phoned, and told us, visiting was Thursday evenings and Saturday afternoons. When he said this we both called him a liar. He said he had heard a tale of me picking her up by her hair. He was asked for proof. He said, 'I only heard'. The clerk said, 'Disregard this'. He asked Mr Field if he thought Shirley was at risk. He replied, 'Definitely yes'.

The court sat on for a long time. Then they said, 'We have given this careful thought. It is an unusual case. The smacking and shaking and hitting with a slipper we disregard. These are common happenings in family life. But we think Shirley needs help. We will give her another month.' (There was no report from Meadowlands.) We stormed out and didn't hear any more. Shirley wasn't in court, because Mr Crosby wouldn't let her come.

After court we told Mr Wilson to meet Peter from school. We told him, 'You have taken the heart out of our family, you might as well take it down brick by brick.' Michael phoned Mr Havelock and told him to keep Peter after school. He called him a two-faced bastard.

We went to see Mr Crosby. He said, 'I thought you would have had her back.' He said, 'I am going to help you work along lines with myself and Mr Wilson, and get some positive action.' We were pleased that someone was willing to help us and Shirley. (Mr Crosby has always been helpful.) . . . He said, 'I am going to let you visit her every day, to help ease the stress all round.' We calmed down. We never get angry with Mr Crosby. Mr Wilson phoned while we were there, and Mr Wilson told him he would meet Peter from school. We saw Shirley for a little while, and told her we would be seeing her every day. She never cried when we left.

Wednesday evening: Mr Wilson came round and we told him what Mr Crosby had said. He said, 'I may not agree with everything Mr Crosby says.' Mr Wilson made it very clear that he didn't want to help us. His visits would only be to find out any flaws or incidents that he could use against us. He cautioned us that he may do this (only because I told them in court they should do this to all their clients).

Thursday: Visited Shirley next day. This was the first time we had seen Shirley anything like her old self. She was laughing, full of nonsense, ruffling Daddy's hair and mauling him around. She still asked to come home and went quiet for a little while, but she only cried for a few minutes.

Mr Crosby told us he had been reprimanded, and told he

was overstepping his mark. He said, 'I won't withdraw my offer. I won't go back on my word, but I may have to at a later date.' We said we understood, and hoped he wouldn't get into trouble for helping us.

The following day the Millers were visted by Mr Wilson. He said he was concerned about Shirley's personality, and that he did not think she would come home at the end of the month, especially after they had stormed out of court in the way they did. He was doubtful about the daily visits, and thought his seniors would disapprove. Mrs Miller warned Shirley they were likely to have to reduce their visits.

Saturday: Both visited Shirley. She wasn't very happy. She kept saying, '*Why* can't I come home, why?' Then she said, 'Auntie Frost says I can come home.' I said, 'I don't think she did.' 'Yes she *did*', she said. Then in the next breath she said, most despairingly, 'No she didn't' [Shirley became more tearful again during subsequent visits.]

Friday 4th December: Mr Wilson came and said they were having a meeting next Wednesday. He said there was a meeting arranged at Meadowlands at 3.45 the next day for us.

The Millers informed their health visitor, Mrs Johnson, of the meeting on the Wednesday, but she was unable to find out the time or place of this meeting from the social services department, so she could not attend it.

Saturday 5th: Visited Shirley. It seemed a very long two hours. She was moody and tearful, and kept asking to go home. She *clung* to Daddy all the time, and *begged* him to take her home.

The meeting consisted of a Mr Hunter [an area principal officer], Mr Pollock, Mr Wilson and Mr Crosby. Mr Hunter hardly gave us a chance to sit down before he started. He seemed determined to let us know he was in charge, and he was going to assert his authority. He was very curt, very abrupt, and downright overpowering. He said, 'I'm *telling you* we are trying for a full care order. I am limiting your

> access to two days a week.' We shouted back at him, 'You wouldn't have this done to your child.' He said, 'Keep my family out of it.' Michael started to storm out. I said, 'No, let's hear some more of this stupid nonsense.' I said, 'I know you're trying to provoke us so you can say we're emotionally unstable.' I asked Mr Crosby twice how much longer he thought he would need with Shirley. Mr Hunter wouldn't let him speak. He said, 'It is nothing to do with Mr Crosby. I'm telling you.' Michael said, 'You're a proper Hitler', and we came home. At least we had seen our enemy for the first time. We thought, 'If the top ones are like that, what chance do we have?'

This account was written by Mrs Miller about two weeks before they were due to attend the further court hearing at which the final decisions about the care order on Shirley and the supervision order on Peter were to be made. At the time when I met them, they were in despair about their chances of making their point of view clear to the court, and were thinking of not even going to court. They felt that as parents their ideas and feelings about their children were unlikely to be considered. I was eventually able to rally their spirits and persuade them to get a solicitor. Up to this point they had not wanted to do this for two reasons. The first was that Mr Miller's work had been so disrupted that he had no money, in spite of his good income over the previous years. Thus he would not qualify for legal aid, yet had no cash to pay a lawyer. The second was because they thought – quite realistically – that very few solicitors would have experience or expertise in this field, and they didn't know who to approach. They had also come to doubt whether anyone would understand their point of view, and even whether it was in any way a valid one. They only approached me through reading something I had written in the local paper, and recognised that I was saying about social services exactly what they felt.

Once they got a solicitor, who was knowledgeable and experienced in this field, Mr and Mrs Miller began to look around for other people who might support their point of view in court. They had been told that the superintendent of Meadowlands. Mr Crosby, 'would have to choose his words carefully, or his job would be at stake'. But they found that Shirley's teachers were only too willing to try to help. The second teacher was most upset when Shirley had been so drastically removed after only three weeks at school, and wanted to give evidence of her good qualities, but was prevented from doing so by the headmaster. The first teacher, who was also a trained psychologist, had left the school, and was quite willing to come to court on the Millers' behalf. It was she who had first been responsible for referring Shirley to the social services department during the summer holidays, but she was appalled at the outcome, and at the use that had been made of her report, which had been misconstrued and built upon quite out of proportion with her intentions. The third witness for the Millers was Shirley's Sunday-school teacher, who was able to report that she had been a regular, attentive and well-behaved member of his class from an early age.

At the final court hearing, the social services department rested most of their case on the behaviour of the Millers towards their various social workers and officials. The evidence of their unsuitability to care for their child had come to depend on an assessment of their reactions to the department that had been trying to remove her. They were said to be volatile, violent and unpredictable. However, their solicitor was able to cast doubt on this and all the other accusations against them, and to call the witnesses – the first teacher, the health visitor and the Sunday-school teacher – who were willing to speak against the social services recommendation. Eventually, the court made a three-year supervision order in respect of Shirley alone. She had already been returned home, on the application of the Millers' solicitor, some two weeks previously. (The final hearing had been adjourned for this period.) Within a week of the court's decision she had gone back to her original school. She attended on a mornings only basis (the Millers' suggestion) and joined a small class, with two young teachers. She settled very easily into this regime, and although she was still insecure and anxious at home, began to make good progress.

I heard from Mrs Miller a year later. Thanks to the efforts of the teachers in the special class, Shirley's behaviour gradually became less boisterous and demanding. In the spring she started to go to school full time. A new social worker was allocated the case, and he liaised especially closely with the teachers, which seemed to benefit Shirley. He also rebuilt relationships with the parents. The family moved out into the country in the autumn, and Shirley was able to take her place in the ordinary class at her new school. Again, the social worker handled the relationship with the new teacher very carefully, so that the change was smoothly made. Shirley has largely ceased to be regarded as a problem child.

It may be worth retracing the elements which contributed to the misunderstandings and conflicts in this story. Shirley was originally referred to social services by her first teacher (during the time when she was attending school part-time) because her mother wanted help with the difficult task of bringing her up. Her mother had had problems with her own physical and mental health – she was overtired and depressed – and Shirley was an exhausting, though also very rewarding, child. Mrs Miller was very frank about her feelings, because she trusted the teacher, and was keen to get any advice and help that was available, mainly for the children's sake.

The first intervention by the social services department treated the referral as a request for very practical assistance. Without a proper assessment (Mrs Miller never spoke to the social worker on her own) Shirley was taken off to three different playgroups. Two of these were much further from her home than she had ever been before – she had never previously been away from her mother for more than a couple of hours at a time. In the process, her arm was broken. The purpose of all this was never explained to Mrs Miller, nor was she consulted. In fact, however well-intentioned this scheme might have been, it provided a very bad basis for the start of Shirley's full-time schooling.

Having given that rather standardised assistance in a clumsy way, but one which gave no hint that they were concerned with underlying family problems, the social services department then reacted as if there was a dangerous crisis. If the first referral was too trivial to discuss with the parents, the second seemed to be too serious. Their approach to pressure applied by the school seems at best uncritical and at worst disrespectful of the parents' rights. The evidence suggests that the headmaster decided at a very early stage, perhaps before her full-time education had begun, that Shirley needed some kind of 'special treatment' that his school could not provide. This opinion was not shared by her first teacher, but this teacher left before the summer holdays. The fact that social services were already involved at a practical level facilitated the setting up of a meeting after Shirley had been at school only three weeks. One of the proposed 'solutions' to the problem of Shirley – a restless five-year-old who lacked concentration and was not ready for school – was to get her into the Sheridan Clinic, a unit situated in an old-style Victorian adult mental hospital, which takes very disturbed and mainly psychotic children. Mr and Mrs Miller knew nothing about this, nor the other possible plans for removing her from school and home.

Most parents assume that their children will receive a normal education as of right unless there is strong evidence that they need special treatment, either because of maladjustment or retardation. Similarly, removing a child from home is a serious step, and parents do not suppose that it can be done without grave grounds for doubt about their capacity. In this case, the headmaster appears to have presented the very early settling difficulties of a five-year-old as signs of disturbance, and the social services department reacted to information passed on by the first teacher as evidence of cruelty. The school's haste to be rid of a demanding newcomer fused with the social services' suspicions of parents. The Millers' rights do not seem to have been considered, and were certainly not explained.

It was not until, rather dazed and confused, they had agreed to Shirley being received into care on a voluntary basis, that the Millers realised that there were more sinister implications behind the authorities' actions. First the headmaster announced that he had no intention of having Shirley back, which had not been made clear at the meeting. Then the ambiguity in the social services department's position begun to emerge. Was Shirley in care for an assessment of her emotional and educational difficulties or to protect her from her cruel parents? Did the department intend to take care proceedings? The Millers got the impression that different members of the department had different intentions – some hostile, others wanting to help Shirley to get on better at school and return to them more happily.

The Millers had had no previous contact with social services, and were predisposed to see social workers as people with some expertise who were coming to help. They not only accepted the department's intervention but welcomed it. They trusted easily and confided fully. They were not disadvantaged people – they were not poor, uneducated or badly accommodated. It is hard to imagine a situation which was better suited to a social worker's intervention of a helpful kind, or to imagine parents who were more helpable. Yet what occurred turned the Millers for a time into hostile and implacable enemies of the social services department. As Mrs Miller's account proceeds, one can note the change from acceptance and frankness to anger and frustration; from seeing them as helpers to seeing them as 'the S.S.' and 'Hitlers'. There was certainly no ideological or political basis for this accusation – it sprang quite spontaneously from their feelings about the way they were treated.

In my conversations with Mr Miller, he put his feelings of bewilderment and confusion in the early stages very vividly.

> I thought they were there to help us. Then all this started – I just didn't understand what it was about. It was as if I might as well not say anything. They didn't listen to a single thing I said. I asked myself, 'Am I her parent? Does what I think matter? Do I have any rights?' They treated me like I was a dangerous enemy. Mr Hunter was like the Gestapo. I sometimes got the impression that the social workers wanted to help, and Mr Crosby did help, but their hands were tied. They couldn't say anything to us because they were acting on instructions from people higher up.'

Mr and Mrs Miller commented that, apart from the headmaster, they found all the other professional people more helpful than the social services staff. Even the policemen seemed much more human and more able to handle the situation from Mrs Miller's account. They also found the residential staff more approachable and more realistic than the field staff. They felt at least they tried to get to know Shirley, rather than to collect scraps of stories and build them up into one black picture, in which they recognised neither Shirley nor themselves.

It is a tribute to the subsequent handling of the case by the new social worker that the Miller's anger (which was compounded with frustration with themselves for having allowed themselves to be 'tricked') and mistrust have subsided. New teachers have achieved a similar good result with Shirley. But these outcomes indicate how unnecessary the very unpleasant and damaging conflicts had been. There can be little point in having social workers to do these very delicate and difficult tasks if they act so insensitively and high-handedly; if they start by delivering services as they might loaves of bread, and end by bullying; if they make no attempt to listen to people, to share their feelings, to recognise their aspirations and their strengths. A department which does not see that it has these obligations to its clients is in some ways a greater threat to civil liberties than an obstructive police force, because its powers are much less defined, and it is dealing in much more intimate and emotionally-charged situations. If social workers are not trying to be helpers, but simply to keep a watchful and suspicious eye on those drawn to their attention, then clients should at least be warned that this is their function. As Mrs Miller said, they should read people a caution.

5
Creative helping

So far most of this book has been about the grim and serious side of helping in social work. It has emphasised the parts of social work to do with sorrow, suffering, cruelty, crime, illness and insanity. It has been about the self-discipline that the social worker needs to give true help to people in these forms of distress. There has been very little about the kind of helping that springs readily from goodwill, that consists in joyful giving, or that leads to warmth and laughter.

This is because I have been very conscious of the dangers of doing harm to people with these problems by offering incomplete or inappropriate help. I have tried to indicate that without the right combination of realism with empathy, the social worker can, often at the invitation of the client, act in a damaging and destructive way. These dangers are very much reduced if the worker is willing to enter the client's world with him, has the courage to recognise all the horrors he sees there, and the endurance to survive them. He needs both the sensitivity to perceive the whole of the client's predicament, and the toughness to help him through it. My theme has been pitfalls of conventional helpfulness, with its tendency to try to keep things nice, friendly, sweet and positive, when in reality they are complex, brutal, bizarre or menacing.

But just because I have not written much about the side of helping that can be spontaneous, creative and joyful, it does not mean that I discount it. In this chapter, I want to turn away from the solemn, unrelenting approach I have so far conveyed. A far lighter touch can be more effective in many situations. Laughter, hopes and strengths can be shared with clients as well as pain, conflicts and weaknesses.

How can the social worker decide when to be grim and serious, and when he can helpfully allow himself to joke and clown? The answer lies mainly in being in tune with the client's feelings. For most people, a visit to a statutory social work agency (especially a first visit) is a pretty painful process. The agency is usually a last resort, where someone goes in despair when family, friends, neighbours and more familiar professionals have failed to help. It is seen as a large and powerful organisation, part of the authoritative state system, and linked to even more awesome institutions like the courts. Furthermore, its 'remedies' are often drastic – care, detention, hospitalisation – even though it also has access to desirable resources – benefits and services. In such a setting, a carefree and cavalier greeting would usually be careless and callous.

Yet without forgetting any of this, the social worker can still stay open to quite different forms of helping from the ones described so far. Even if the ultimate basis of his work lies in the kind of realism and honesty that I have tried to illustrate, he does not have to keep grinding away in this low gear, as if the whole road was uphill. Indeed, to do so would show just the sort of inflexible, one-sided approach that I have criticised throughout this book. He needs to be alive to other notions of the sources of help.

The need for this became very clear to me when I was able to see the same problems from two perspectives, one inside social work, the other outside. Seen from the social work perspective, people needed help based on a determined uncovering of the underlying issues, in which the worker took responsibility of reaching the essentials. Seen from the other, they could be helped by the whole-hearted support of a group of like-minded people in similar trouble. Both were often equally effective. The same person could get as much help from a sensitive but strong-minded social worker and from joining with others struggling to assert their identity, and to resist labelling, blame and scorn.

The second perspective I got from my experience of working for several years with a claimants union. In the union, which was for people claiming social security or other state benefits, many of my most valued and trusted colleagues had been clients of mine at one time or another, and many more had been clients of other social workers. But the way in which we shared our day-to-day union tasks was quite unlike the sort of sharing I have described in other examples. It was practical, immediate and purposeful, and it gave rise to strong feelings of solidarity, loyalty and significance, so that even the trivial and irritating could become a source of amusement or inspiration. All our members suffered the gross disadvantages and petty pinpricks of claiming for a living. By providing support, company and solace for each other, we improved the quality of life for our active members, and provided practical help for many others. These regular contacts and commitments gave rise to other, more personal forms of help. People shared family problems and private worries, so that the scope of helping was far wider than the original focus. What we eventually produced was a close-knit network of assistance and emotional support which was capable of helping with almost all the difficulties social workers tackle, and some they do not.

Yet our whole approach could not have been more contrasted with social work. We set out quite consciously to avoid being 'welfare advisers'. This was especially relevant when we got hold of an office. Obviously, it was a valuable focus for our meetings and other activities; but we feared that we would tend to sit about in it rather than get out to places where we could be more useful – the social security office, for instance. We also feared that more active members would be seen as experts who knew everything, and soon the whole ethos of the union – that every claimant should help every other – would be destroyed. So we made a rule that we would always encourage as many people as came into the office to stay around to meet each other, to use it as a place to talk and drink coffee. Then if a new person came in, he would not be taken aside by one 'expert' member and asked what help he needed. He would be introduced to everyone, and it would be explained that everyone's advice was valuable, because no one had experienced every social security problem, though everyone had experienced quite a few. If he needed to be accompanied to the office, this meant there was usually quite a choice of supporters and representatives. The new member felt he was joining an active group, not applying to yet another welfare agency, or getting yet more professional help.

In the same spirit, we tried to turn the local social security waiting room into a friendly place, where people would be sure of being welcomed by their fellow claimants if not by the staff behind the counter. There were always two union representatives there to offer help and support with claims, especially where emergency payments over the counter were needed. But we did not do this in an official or confidential way. We talked quite loudly, were friendly, laughed a lot, and often involved everyone in comments about the absurdity of the situations all claimants faced every day. Most waiting rooms in social security offices are grim places, and people seldom speak to each other. The chairs all face one way, and are bolted to the floor. Claimants arrive feeling anxious, angry or desperate. They are on edge or impatient. They often feel they are competing with each other for scarce funds and for the time of staff who are rushed and harrassed. Sometimes claimants criticise each other, and even fights are not unknown. But we were able to change all that very quickly. Our waiting room was a place where people shared conversation, cigarettes and food, where we talked about the union's policies and plans, arranged meetings, exchanged information, looked after each other's children. Even the staff eventually recognised and welcomed the improved atmosphere. Claimants behaved more humanly because, as well as feeling they would get support in getting their rights, they were enabled to relax, even to enjoy themselves. The spirit of helpfulness spread to neighbouring unemployment benefit offices, and even where the union had no organised representation, claimants spontaneously gave each other assistance and advice.

It was the first rule of the union that we supported all claimants without distinction or reservation. Without this wholehearted commitment, we felt we risked duplicating and reinforcing the social security policy of trying to discriminate between the deserving and the undeserving. If we were seen as suspicious or prying, we would intensify the sense of stigma and the shame that made some claimants so timid or so hostile. As a result, people were very frank with us about the complexity of their problems, both personal and financial. Instead of restricting themselves to an account which they felt would present themselves as 'deserving', they told us all the details of their difficulties. As a result, we were able to get them and give them much more effective help.

In most of the people we met, the extent of this need was far greater than they had previously revealed to social security or anyone else. But even in the few examples we encountered of claimants overstating their need in a misleading way, this was usually transparent and hilarious. Mr Peterson (see chapter 3) arrived one day very drunk and loud. 'I've just come off a boat from Newquay', he shouted. 'They know perfectly well you've just walked up from Codport', I muttered to him, encouraging him to sit down. 'Look here Bill', he retorted at the top of his considerable voice, 'I'll tell the lies, you're only here to back me up'.

My own motivation for working with the union was partly political, and our activities certainly had political implications. We were able to influence social security policy very considerably at a local level, and we kept our town's office open when it was scheduled for closure under a national plan. We also brought many local social issues to the public eye, and influenced political responses to them. But the longer I was with the union, the more I appreciated the parts of our work which were similar in aims and results to what I was doing as a probation officer. By entirely different methods, we strengthened people's sense of identity, gave their lives coherence and meaning. When we took someone's claim on appeal to a tribunal, it didn't always matter how much we won, or even if we won. The feeling of drift, the nagging doubt, the bitterness, the sense of injustice, had all been sapping the claimant's morale. The experiences of presenting a case convincingly, of making a social security decision look mean and shabby, of belonging to a group which was not ashamed of being claimants, were often enough to alter someone's outlook. Many later told us that this was the beginning of a great change for the better in their fortunes.

I was taking part in the union's activities in my 'spare time', and not as the probation officer I then was. Nearly everybody in the union knew the job I did, and few seemed to hold it against me, though some said it gave them pause at first. It was interesting to see how few problems members considered were outside the scope of the group's own helpfulness. The only ones that were referred to me for my professional expertise were all either serious marital difficulties or matters of acute mental illness. Apart from those, I played much the same part as others in the round of activities and discussions which made up the help the union gave.

What I hope I learnt from all this for my social work practice was that wherever possible I should take opportunities to put clients in touch with each other, and to assist them in forming purposeful groups. This I tried to do, not just on the basis of common social disadvantages, but also on an *ad hoc* basis. I have already given the example of Tony's homecoming from prison (Chapter 4). Later, when I worked in the psychiatric hospital, I found I was visiting a number of young, intelligent and interesting ex-patients, all of whom were socially isolated. I was talking to each in turn about why he or she found it so difficult to meet others with whom they had anything in common, or to join a group. Eventually one evening I just drove from one to the other, picked them all up, and took them to a pub. Nearly a year later, this group still meets fortnightly, and has steadily expanded its membership.

In many ways, the more serious and socially stigmatised the client's problems, the more he is likely to benefit from the support of a group of others in similar circumstances. Yet often the social worker in a statutory agency will find it difficult to refer someone straight to such a group. This is because of the danger that the client may experience this as being fobbed off, not taken seriously. The social worker needs to be careful that he listens to the essentials in the client's story, identifies areas where he can help, and fully explains the purpose and ethos of the group.

Yet when I worked with the claimants union, we detected an ambivalence among social workers about referring clients to us which did not seem to stem from this factor alone. Part of their resistance was probably to do with our political activities, and our reputation for outspokenness and direct action. Social workers often have a disproportionate fear of conflict, especially when there is a risk of this conflict being with their own agency, or other public services. They underestimate the benefits of a vigorous debate, and of counter-pressure by those who have traditionally been underdogs and powerless. They seem to fear that if disadvantaged people get together, their anger and destructiveness will know no bounds. Yet in fact, belonging to an organisation, and the experience of exerting enough pressure to force the authorities to hear their point of view, allow people's frustrations to be expressed in less destructive ways. The other fear, that clients will be exploited as pawns by unscrupulous trouble-makers, is one that social workers are seldom prepared to take the trouble to investigate. By accompanying their clients to such groups, they could quickly evaluate them. Instead, they tend to play safe, to negotiate with authority on a client's behalf, over his head, often leaving him feeling more powerless and confused than before.

Another fear among social workers seems to be that when groups of clients get together they 'collude' with each other, giving support to views of problems which, even if they are not militant, are one-sided and simplistic. This seems to me to be largely based on a misunderstanding of the difference between the kind of help social workers give people, and the kind they give each other. In my experience, people with common problems make very shrewd and complex assessments of each other, but they tend to communicate these to each other in covert or non-verbal ways. In their dealings with outsiders, they emphasise the solidarity, trust and goodwill between them, because this is the whole basis of their help. The recognition of each other's value and strengths is given primary importance, is explicit and unequivocal. In private, they may disagree and confront each other more toughly than any social worker could. But public support, especially in relation to authority, is of crucial significance in breaking out of a vicious circle of shame and resentment. The group will usually accept a direct, honest and realistic approach by the social worker or other official to its member, so long as this acknowledges and respects his dignity, and that of the group itself.

The danger of unrealistic collusion seems to me to be far greater when a group of clients meet together under the aegis of a social worker. From my observation, this is specially the case in a therapeutic setting. When the helping processes between clients are formalised – as for instance in a therapeutic community – a kind of falseness can develop. The client group can parody the host institution, imitating the least helpful aspects of its methods, aping its jargon, copying its mannerisms. The natural and healthy processes of helping can become subordinate to superficial and spurious ones in an intense atmosphere of hothouse intrigue. Unless the staff work very hard to preserve an ethos of honesty and openness, the characteristic atmosphere can become precious and petty, with over-dramatised good works paraded for the public gaze. In such settings, real help is still given by clients to each other, but usually humbly and unobtrusively, away from the limelight, and often by the most 'disturbed' people, who are least tolerated by the others.

In the hospital ward where I now work, such an atmosphere does from time to time prevail. Patients become self-indulgent in their concern about their problems and their relations with each other. Yet often their sense of the ridiculous in all this is only just beneath the surface, and, so long as staff do not get drawn into such over-intensity, this will frequently break through. The manifestations of mental illness are often funny, and the paraphernalia for its treatment can be funnier still. The ward notice board provides scope for patient humour – a spoof guide to ward routine, bogus prescriptions for staff, therapeutic instructions for a football team, a photograph of a notorious con-man carrying the inscription, 'Would you buy a used car from this man? If so, ring Bishopstone 41933.'

The ward meetings are the sort of set-pieces that encourage self-dramatisation and falseness, but occasionally a patient will, by sheer simplicity or force of character, cut through all this, and let in a breath of fresh air. If the staff are not threatened by such a person, he can be as therapeutic as Randle P. McMurphy would have been in *One Flew Over the Cuckoo's Nest* if he had been given his head. One such patient, a tough-looking, plain-spoken, outdoor man, was elected chairman of the ward meetings, and at once all the precious nonsense went out of them. People talked and laughed who had previously been gloomy and withdrawn. He was specially popular with some of the patients who had previously been quiet and low in the pecking order. On one occasion, when he was wearing a T-shirt emblazoned with the number 69, he had the following exchange with an excited little middle-aged lady, who had heard of his prowess, but whether at football or something else was not clear.

'That number 69, is it your favourite position?'
'Oh yes, definitely.'
'And do you play out there on the field?'
'Well, only when the grass is dry.'
'And why do you specially like number 69?'
'Well, if you look carefully, you'll see that it's the same each way up.'

Such interludes suggest that there is some truth in the old notion that a sense of proportion about emotional problems is best preserved by laughter and humour. Yet the social worker can seldom carry such easy and spontaneous good nature into his dealings with clients, at least in the first stages of their meeting. Because of his official connections, he would be insensitive to draw too much attention to the funny side of his client's situation. If he was too quick to seek common ground in humour, he might be tempted to 'jolly along' people who were really depressed or desperate, which would probably be exactly what others had tried unsuccessfully to do before.

Very often, the best way to reach the client's sense of the absurd is through an awareness of the absurdity of one's own position. The fact is that, in their distress or in attempts to evade what they most fear, clients often put social workers into very odd situations. They put pressure on them to do silly things, and often get them to act in strange ways. If the social worker catches a mood of panic, for instance, he may find himself rushing about from here to there on wild errands of mercy, with his car full of children, animals, furniture or old rubbish. If only he could slow down enough to see how silly he was being, he might be able to point this out to the client, who, in laughing at him, may come to laugh at himself.

Sometimes the situation is even more bizarre. On one occasion, a rather grand lady who had been a patient in the mental hospital, and had married another patient who used to be a butler, asked me to come and discuss some difficulties in their relationship. To my amazement, I was served a formal dinner, with wine; while he waited at table, she ate with me and made cultured conversation. As the meal ended, they started to have an absurdly stagey row. He put on his coat to leave in a huff (as if to seek to give more satisfaction elsewhere). As I sat there folding my napkin, I pointed out how difficult it was for me to comment helpfully on their problems from the position of a polite dinner guest, and how remarkably silly I felt. At this their sense of the ridiculous began to return, and I pointed out how I felt as if I was cast in a role in rather bad drawing-room comedy, and how they, too, were playing not very well-scripted parts. In the end, we all managed to sit down and have a fairly sensible discussion.

On other occasions, my own reaction has been a quite inappropriate expression of the pressure I felt from the client. One time I found myself sitting in a rather bleak office listening to a man recounting all the dreary and depressing features of his life. Since he had come out of hospital he had lost his job, split up with his girlfriend, moved into a dismal room. He was saying things like, 'I can't take much more, Bill. I've reached the end of the road. I can't see any way forward. I'm in a fog, Bill. I just don't know what to do.' At this point, he lit a cigarette, and then went across the room to fetch an ashtray, which he put carefully on a table, just out of reach of where he was sitting. Then he sat back and resumed his tale of misery, failure and defeat, while the ash on the end of his cigarette grew longer and longer. Eventually I could stand it no more. I jumped up and moved the whole table nearer him, so the ashtray was within his reach. Then I said, 'Look what you just made me do!' By drawing attention to my own irrational impulse, I was able to go on to discuss the pressure he constantly put on me to endorse things I couldn't agree with, to help him in ways that weren't helpful, and to do things he didn't really need done.

Other clients have put me in impossible positions by confiding what could not possibly be kept confidential, or by placing me between themselves and someone else they feared. Here again, I have felt the only thing to do was to draw attention to the absurdity of the situation. 'What am I supposed to do or say about that?' 'What sort of a position does this put me in?' Often I will then go on to illustrate how I feel about where I have been left. I will act the part of myself meeting whoever it is I am supposed to meet, knowing and not knowing what I am supposed not to know and not to tell. 'Oh hello, Mr X, I was just talking to your wife the other day and . . .' Or I will act the part of a comic and ineffective bodyguard, or whatever. This seems the only way forward in such a situation.

Sometimes the crisis is more immediate. A student once told a class of mine how compromised he had felt when he reluctantly agreed with a middle-aged lady who had been placed on probation that he would temporarily collude with her in keeping this secret from her husband. On one of his visits the husband arrived home unexpectedly from work to find them in deep and intense discussion of her emotional problems. He was made to feel embarrassed and guilty, and to act the part of a sort of ambiguous and apologetic out-of-hours milkman. In discussion, the class felt it would have been possible, and more constructive, after the initial fudged introductions, to point out to the lady that he had been put in an embarrassing situation because she hadn't explained before to her husband why he was visiting her. He would then have had to hope that she would tell him the truth about this straight away, before he jumped to other conclusions.

Yet there may be other times when the social worker is put in an ignominious position and all he can do is try to grin and bear it. One example again concerned Mr Peterson. He used sometimes to come into town to get drunk, and ring up more for the lift home than anything else. One market day he rang me when I was home for tea. I said I would meet him in the bus station a few minutes later. I found him leaning against a wall in a busy concourse, bemoaning his fate. 'I can't go on, Bill, I can't take any more. I'm better off inside. At least the Governor always gives me a decent job.' He rocked precariously to and fro in his nautical garb, like a bosun in a high wind. At this point Jackie, a young woman who was also under my supervision, walked by with her three-year-old daughter. The little girl detached herself from her mother and started to swing on my leg, shrieking in a high-pitched voice, 'Sweeties Jordan, I want some sweeties!' I suggested to the swaying mariner that we should go into the bus station cafe for a cup of tea, and we staggered off with the little girl still shrilly in tow. The cafe was very full, and we jostled a few elbows and sloshed a few cups as we lurched towards the counter. While Mr Peterson was ordering his refreshment, the little girl kept wailing that she couldn't see the sweeties, so I hoisted her up to give her a better view. Suddenly she was snatched from my grasp by a furious mother (who must have lost track of her in the crowds) indignantly shouting, 'What the hell are you doing with my child?' Fifty heads swivelled and shocked looks bored into me. Drunken sailor and blushing child molester found themselves seats as quickly as possible.

I believe that social workers have to be prepared to make fools of themselves from time to time, and to be made fools of by others too. A probation colleague once described his role very vividly as being 'God's Fool'. If a social worker spends his time trying to safeguard himself against being made to look ridiculous, he is likely to limit his opportunities for giving real help to his clients. It is better to let the ridiculous happen, and then try to use it creatively; or failing that, simply to endure it.

There are other ways in which shared laughter can be part of the helping process. Working in a mental hospital, one could often be excused for thinking that some patients have no sense of humour. Acutely anxious and depressed people lose touch with their appreciation of the absurd, yet often they do have much more capacity for fun than anyone meeting them in such a ward could imagine. After my tough confrontations with Beryl and Margaret (Chapter 3) when their worst anxieties were faced, both were able to laugh with me, particularly about those occasions. Beryl would remember gleefully 'the time when you sat on the floor', and Margaret would smile to herself when I referred to her more outrageous fears. In both examples, when later anxieties arose, I could refer back to those formative crisis points, and this helped preserve a sense of proportion. Both saw the funny side of themselves at their worst, and neither wanted to be so silly again. Both could get their subsequent fears in perspective against this extreme version of their anxieties.

There is something of an art in finding shorthand phrases which can refer back to such incidents in ways which make them seem both funny and safe. If the social worker can help the client find a joking way of seeing his past nightmares, it may even serve as one way of enabling him to master things that once terrified him.

But it is not only by humour that this process of obtaining some kind of mastery over anxieties can be achieved. Sometimes the same thing can be done by helping the client be able just to describe the previously inexpressible, to find words and images for frightening feelings and fantasies. This can be one of the most creative processes of social work, as the worker imaginatively enters the client's inner world, and gets an intuitive grasp of its landscape and contours, its population and politics.

I worked with a girl recently who had been a very deprived child. She had been brutally treated by her parents, humiliated, told she was stupid and backward, and rejected. She had been educated in special schools and cared for in institutional surroundings. On leaving school she had gone on working in similar settings, and been unable to break from her deprived past. She was frustrated, but violently ambivalent about changing. She felt she would lose her identity if she became 'normal', yet she resented her past. Without what made her different, she feared she would be lost, be nobody. When she talked about herself she showed a glimpse of her hurt, then covered up angrily again. The second time she came into hospital, I tried to convey to her what it felt like to talk to her. I said she seemed like an armed guard at the gate of a palace that was also her. Her problem was the jewel inside the palace. I was like a tourist, a visitor. I was allowed in at certain special times to see the jewel, but not to touch, not to approach too closely even, or the guard would threaten me with his spear. In any case, it would soon be time to leave again. The tour would be over, and I would only have seen the one gem, not the palace. She smiled at this, as if it meant something to her. Later in the same conversation she said, 'I have only given you the *titles* of my problems.' Yet she seemed to have achieved something important just by giving them titles, for this was not the prelude to a long and tortured inner exploration. Indeed, within a few weeks she left the hospital, married, and is now living 'in the normal world' successfully for the first time.

The intuitive and imaginative process I have tried to illustrate is certainly not the only way to help people who feel trapped, either by distorting relationships or by their own mental processes. There are other ways in which they can be helped to achieve a sense of release from the straitjacket of repetitive thoughts or limited emotional responses. I often adopt a much more active approach to try to help clients break out of the corner they have put themselves into.

One such method is to encourage the client to experience all the elements in his imprisoning situation, whether these are aspects of himself or of other people. This is a very free adaptation of the techniques of gestalt therapy. I ask the client to become the different parts of himself (conscience and free spirit, old man and youth, kill-joy and playboy) or to be both himself and his oppressor in turn. I encourage him to act out the different parts, to enact the drama with gesture and posture as well as in dialogue, to feel as well as to speak, and to carry the whole thing right through to its conclusion, however painful and alarming. The objective is to bring into the present a frightening encounter that has been suppressed or left unfinished, and to go through an experience that has been postponed because of its risks. By becoming the various elements in his conflicts, the client seems, sometimes almost magically, to be freed to think and act on new and more creative lines.

I first tried this approach with Nigel, a middle-aged man of good intelligence, who had a formidable history of psychiatric treatment, including several mental hospital admissions, for a host of symptoms, some physical, but mainly connected with obsessional fears. He was unhappily married and had a very delinquent son, whom I had supervised years previously when I was a probation officer. Nigel was a strange mixture, for although he was a handsome and charming man, and often used this to his advantage, he could be amazingly obtuse, stuffy and boring, and singularly lacking in insight about himself. In my first interview with him, he used rather pompous phrases like, 'One tends to do this,' and generalised a good deal in a sanctimonious manner about other people's lives and morals. I suggested at the end of this unproductive conversation that there should be some ground rules for our future meetings, such as that he should always say 'I feel x' or preferably 'I feel x now', and never generalise. Nigel picked up the point of this straight away, and corrected himself in future whenever he broke these rules.

One difficulty of introducing the technique I am about to describe is its artificiality. This makes the client feel self-conscious, but also the worker. In explaining the method to Nigel, I admitted that I felt diffident and embarrassed, and would continue to feel these things until we had got into the swing of it. To my surprise and pleasure Nigel welcomed the new approach. He had talked about his problems for years, and the chance to do something active was a nice change. We identified several different aspects of himself which had emerged in his conversations with me and which were quite inconsistent with each other – for instance, the stuffy father-figure and a rebellious teenager who still (in his fifties) believed he could make it as a singing star! Also, there was an old man who was a lonely tramp. Nigel became each of these in turn, but there was no dialogue or connection between them. Our sessions became much more dynamic when Nigel talked about his parents for the first time. Both had died in unhappy circumstances, and he had failed to make his peace with either. I encouraged Nigel to talk to each of his parents in turn, to have a final conversation with them, to reply as each of them to himself, and to say goodbye. He did this, and it was a very emotional yet satisfying and complete experience. He wept a great deal, then felt exhausted and at peace. Later he visited their graves for the first time (years after their deaths). Soon after this, Nigel announced he was ready to leave the hospital. He told the consultant that he had realised there were more important things to do in life than check electricity switches. This was two years ago, and he has not returned for treatment. When I last bumped into him, he had just started his first job for many years.

The artificiality of this method is also one of its advantages. All therapies are somewhat artificial, and rely on strange conventions and an odd relationship between patient and therapist. In many ways it is better if this is made explicit. Although the client is initially apprehensive and self-conscious, he works his way out of it. This is preferable, in my view, to a method which masquerades as being like ordinary conversation, where the relationship appears to be on commonsense terms, and then there is a sudden denouement, when the hidden agenda is revealed and the therapist emerges in his true colours.

In many ways the artificiality of this method mirrors and confronts the strangely contrived and theatrical nature of many mental problems. The mind seems to follow odd conventions rather like 'the unities' of the seventeenth century French theatre. Under these rules the play had to be a continuous set-piece; switches and jumps of time and space were prohibited; no action, no conflict, no death must take place on stage, so nothing was ever seen, completed and laid to rest. This method of work might be compared with Victor Hugo's plays; it directly challenges the rules, by playing tricks of time and geography, and it insists that action be carried through to its conclusion. The result is that what is so apparently artificial and stagey emerges as very moving and real. The client experiences something which is more emotionally draining and satisfying and ultimately more true than his constrained and limited suffering.

Another example will illustrate some different features of this method. John, a plumber in his mid-thirties, had just been divorced by his wife. He had had a stormy marriage, and one previous hospital admission, but he had been devoted to his children. He was a heavy drinker, and regarded by the nursing staff as a rather sinister character, who stirred up trouble and was not averse to using violence to settle quarrels. But John appeared to me as someone in the grip of a fatal mixture of guilt and resentment. He was so torn between blame of himself for the breakup of his marriage, and fury with his wife for rejecting him, that he had reached a point of paralysis and standstill. He couldn't work, he couldn't live alone, he couldn't bring himself to see his children, he couldn't even meet his parents. He shook a good deal, slept badly, felt in a daze, even though the separation had taken place six months before. I started by getting him to hold a conversation with his children in which he was both himself and them. He found this very difficult, but it enabled him at least to write to them. Then he spoke of persistent and terrifying dreams he had, in which he was haunted by his wife. In one of these she walked towards him up the street, becoming larger and larger, and eventually crushing him under her foot like a beetle. He would wake up terrified, sweating, sometimes on the floor. He was so frightened he couldn't even go into the dormitory without shaking. I encouraged him to act out the elements in another frightening dream. He arrived at home to visit his children, but at once his wife appeared. She started to poke at him with her fingers and accuse him vindictively, reminding him of everything he had done wrong. He fled in terror, jumped into his car, and started to drive away. To his horror he found his wife beside him in the car. At this point John became his wife. With hatred and malice she brought up all John's misdeeds. When I asked her what she was doing she said bitterly, 'I'm being John's conscience. I'm going to stay with him wherever he goes for the rest of his life. I'm going to make sure he suffers. I'm never going to let him forget.' This continued for a full half-hour. Eventually feeling drained myself (although I had hardly spoken) I said to John that I thought we should stop. He did not seem to hear me, and I had to say it again, more loudly and clearly. He then appeared to emerge, as from a trance, and started to cough and sweat. He said he felt terrible, as if a very tight coil had been around his chest and neck. His mouth was dry, and when he had rubbed himself enough to recover, he needed to drink several glasses of water. I did not talk much about what had happened, and he did not remember much, apparently. I do not find it helpful to pick over such sessions with the client, certainly not to interpret them – the experience itself is the meaningful and helpful thing. John was shaken and physically upset straight afterwards, and needed time to recover, but the change in him the following day was remarkable. He started to sleep soundly, eat well and take exercise. He quickly arranged to see his children, and made a success of this. Some weeks later he left the hospital, having fallen in love with another patient, whom he has since married. They overcame very considerable adversities, found accommodation, and are both doing very well a year later.

It is an unfortunate aspect of several of the specialised therapeutic schools that they sometimes seem to imply that only the relatively 'mature' and articulate can benefit from their methods. The result is almost an impression that such techniques are only of use to fellow therapists and others with professional backgrounds, and not to clients – certainly not to clients of statutory agencies. In spite of the very important contribution of such ideas as gestalt therapy, encounter groups, psychodrama, transactional analysis and so on, they have had relatively little influence in social work practice. Yet the 'growth movement' flourishes in the private sector, and many social workers pay large fees to benefit from the insights and experiences of these methods. Some advocates of these methods have even argued that the only 'real' help that can be given must necessarily be outside the state system, because its organisational constraints and bureaucratic structure impose such barriers to creativity, and its clients are such unpromising material.

I have a number of strong objections to these arguments, some of which I shall put in the final chapter. But on purely practical grounds, I find them unconvincing. It is just not true that creative work cannot be done in statutory services. If a worker has the confidence to experiment, the trust in his clients, and the ability to inspire trust in them, there are opportunities every day for work along these lines. Many of the barriers to creativity exist in the minds of social workers, not in the organisations that employ them. It is the workers who need to maintain a distinction between what is good for and practicable with clients, and what is good for themselves. They attribute to their agencies their own doubts about sharing with clients, about exposing themselves, about treating clients as true equals. They use pressure of other work and of time and of agency procedure to exclude clients from the benefits of these techniques, yet they still find time for themselves to benefit from them.

I realised last year that I could take the doctors' opinions that a patient was 'just an anxious housewife', or 'someone who should really be on a conventional ward' or 'one of those people who gets worse if she talks about her problems' as a positive indicator for these methods. These opinions were, in effect, consigning the patient to the scrapheap, as not mature, clever and articulate enough, or too anxious and inflexible, to benefit from group or individual psychotherapy. What I found was that such patients responded very favourably to methods which used action as much as words, which employed movement, posture, the body. They quickly got the point of talking to their legs and answering back as their legs. They revelled in the opportunity to be their dogmatic husbands, or their moaning mothers. They were only too happy to escape from the constraints of the patient role, where they were cast as their miserable, inhibited selves. Some of my best results with these methods have been with such clients.

There is one other approach which I have not mentioned, but which I certainly do not reject. This is based on learning theory, and adapted from behaviour modification. I have reservations about the extent to which in the classical version of this approach, the therapist is cast as an expert, a technician, who sets the patient tasks. But I do use the principles of this method, as I have already illustrated in the example of Margaret (Chapter 3). In that case, it was very helpful, in addition to using some of the exercises based on the method just described, to draw up a list of the things Margaret most feared, and to set her and Jack the task of practising these, starting with the easiest first.

But I used this approach in a more thoroughgoing way in one of my cases when I was a probation officer. Mr and Mrs O'Rourke had five sons and two daughters. One of the sons was on probation to me, and I got to know them all well over a period of years. Mr O'Rourke was short, stocky, aggressive, heavy-drinking, and extremely inarticulate. Mrs O'Rourke was kind, generous and longsuffering. But there was an angry side of her which emerged in her son's resistance to his father, and a confused and guilty side of him which I caught glimpses of from time to time. I saw them occasionally after the probation order ended, but one night there was a crisis. Mr O'Rourke had got drunk on his holiday money; Mrs O'Rourke had fled from his anger and violence. In the aftermath of this there was a good deal of recrimination, but mainly in low key. Eventually, Mrs O'Rourke shyly mentioned that she blamed herself for her husband's drinking and violence, because of longstanding sexual difficulties. They agreed to see me regularly for a time to discuss these, and over a period of about two months I listened to a rather moving account of how her feelings about sex had been altered after a sterilisation that she had not wanted, and how he had tried to be tolerant of the subsequent physical coolness and distance between them. But after all their honesty about the emotional component in this story they were still in separate bedrooms, and Mrs O'Rourke couldn't bring herself to start to have any kind of sexual relationship again, even though she wanted to for both their sakes. I then put it to them that we had talked very helpfully about their problem, but that there was another whole approach to it which we had not tried, which was on quite different principles. I explained that I was not at all confident in my own ability to work in this way, but that I thought they ought to understand its methods so that they could choose whether they wanted to try it. I then explained a regime which started with them sharing a room, in separate beds for a time, then progressed to sharing a bed, then to touching, and finally to intercourse. They were both very keen to try this. I explained the need to take time over each stage, and how Mrs O'Rourke must have the option to withdraw to a previous stage at any point if she became upset or frightened. I explained that we would draw up a list of the stages and a timetable, and that my visits would be to check on progress and talk about any problems that arose. In fact, the whole process was considerably shortened by their rapid movement through the stages in about a fortnight, a piece of news which Mr O'Rourke conveyed to me mainly by a series of grunts and gestures, and Mrs O'Rourke confirmed with smiles and nods. The only bad moment in the whole process had been my taking fright at Mr O'Rourke's suggestion that we should drink to the success of it on the first night they were to share a bed. The sight of the bottle of whisky he produced made me very anxious that he might not keep to the rules, and I suggested that both he and I should have time out from drinking that night. Indeed, I was pretty anxious throughout the whole thing, and told them so, confessing that it was all based on what I had read in books and not on experience, but they were very kind and reassuring, and obviously appreciated a form of help they could readily understand and apply.

I have described a number of different methods of helping based on what are usually considered as rival schools of thought. I have suggested that to be most effective, a social worker needs a range of responses that come fairly naturally to him, that enable him to be flexible and imaginative in his reactions to his clients' problems. All these depend on an intuitive grasp of the essentials in the client's predicament, communication of the purposes of the methods suggested, and the creation of an atmosphere of trust and goodwill. Without these things, all this technique will seem like so much gimmickry. If the client feels that the worker is simply seeing him in terms of a pre-set theoretical framework, or imposing something alien on him, or experimenting with him or using him for some other purpose, he is unlikely to cooperate or benefit. The worker needs to be seen as a credible and helpful person, not as a mere technical expert. But exactly the same considerations apply to 'traditional' methods of social work. These are just as foreign to clients, just as mysterious and suspect, as these new-fangled ones, and just because they are familiar to the social worker, this does not mean that they are not frightening to the client.

I always tell clients when I am trying something new, or when I feel unsure of whether it will help them, and I always confess to doubts and embarrassments about using artificial methods. I think this is not only more honest but also more helpful. Otherwise it is made to look as if all the resistance is in the client, when often much is in the worker. Also, I always respect a client's refusal to go along with something that is new and strange. I do not challenge it unless it is obviously evasive and based on a bogus excuse. Often, when a client rejects one form of help he initiates another, or finds his own solution to his problem.

In using a number of different methods, I hope I am never guilty of the sort of maddening eclecticism that sometimes bedevils social work. This is the habit of reducing every new idea and technique to the same grey mash, insisting that it's all the same really, and taking the spark of life from it by applying only the incidentals in the most superficial way. This approach accommodates new methods by making them safe, defusing them of their originality and creativity, showing they are no better or worse than anything else by using them without imagination or verve.

Instead, I would hope to extract the essential principles from new ideas, and adapt them to my own style of working. I want to use these principles, but through myself. I want to get inside them, or get them inside me. I want to be able to get across to clients what they are about and what I am about. I do not want to wear them like a suit of armour that makes me impregnable but clumsy. I would rather make a mistake and admit I was wrong.

Very often clients pick up the principles behind a method of work even when I have not spelled them out, and they are able to use it for themselves. Nigel certainly did so, and would often anticipate my ideas, or go beyond what I had told him in applying them. But more strikingly Margaret (who was so intensely anxious that she hardly seemed to take anything in) applied a remarkably pure version of behaviour modification to her daughter's sleeping problems. She and Jack went out and bought her a bed, allowing her to choose it. They then told her it was hers, but she must sleep in it, so they would have to lock her door if she did not. Applying in reverse the same principle as I had used with them, they survived her lengthy tantrum the first night, and by the third no longer needed to lock the door. All this they told me after they had succeeded; they certainly didn't get the idea directly from me.

There is much waste in social work as a result of conflicts between the different schools of thought and practice. Subscribing to one school can mean cutting off from a whole range of techniques that can be of real help to clients. There is some spurious security and satisfaction for the worker in the sense of belonging to something, in the certainty of ideology and the suppression of doubt. But the loss of flexibility and creativity is in the long run a loss to the social worker as well as the client.

I find that the great challenge of social work is how ideas as various as my political ideals, my ideas about communities, about families, relationships, about personal frustrations and satisfactions, can all be translated into help that clients can use. Some of these ideas are seemingly very abstract; others very immediate and sensory. Some started from reading and thinking, others were built on personal experience. But all the things I believe or feel strongly about ought in some way to be available to the people I am trying to help. To cut them off from these sources of strength and excitement is ultimately also to fragment and impoverish my own working life.

However odd or repugnant a new idea may seem, I hope I try to understand it, then grasp it, to keep worrying at it until I get something from it. I am sure clients sense when a social worker has shut up shop, and stopped searching for himself and others. They must pick up the feeling that they are talking to someone who has heard it all before, who has made up his mind, who is simply putting them in one of the categories of his past experience. I have learnt a great deal from my clients, and I hope I still have much more to learn.

6
Helping and organisations

In this final chapter I want to return to the questions raised right at the beginning of the book. How are the personal processes of helping in social work that I have tried to describe relevant to the social problems which are so widespread in our society? How can good social work be done in organisations big enough to meet such large-scale needs? What is the role of social work in a welfare state?

So far in this book I have argued for and illustrated an approach to helping which is small-scale and personal, and which requires the social worker to use the whole of himself in all-round attention to the whole of his client. I have written of communication between the middles of people and of trying to reach the essentials of the client's personality and situation – implying a depth and totality of attention by the social worker. All this is open to the objection that such a notion of helping has no part to play in a welfare state whose primary purpose is to guarantee minimum standards of material provision for all its citizens, and special services for those with particular needs.

Yet my own first allegiance is to such a welfare state rather than to social work. It seems to me that the first priority of social policy in any civilised society should be a decent and secure life for all, and the humane care of its physically and socially handicapped citizens. Compassionate relationships are no substitutes for an adequate income and a comfortable home. Good education and health care are much more important to the life chances of the great majority of people than anything social work might give them.

Yet there are social services, which I believe the state should provide, whose quality depends on the personal relationships between those who give them and those who receive them. This is not true of income maintenance or housing, and both education and health, while they entail personal relationships, also crucially involve other skills. The point about the services I am concerned with is that they can only be good services if they are given in a certain way – sensitively, and with a generous offer of individual attention. They are no less part of the Welfare State for this, and they should be available to all who need them. Yet the detailed means by which they are given are as important as their organisation and planning, and these two aspects of their provision are often closely linked in problematic ways.

What I am suggesting is that social work help is not so much a service in itself as a way of giving certain services. Without this ingredient, these services will not be of good quality, no matter how well they are organised. Yet without its links with these services and their organisation, social work has little relevance to the lives of the majority of people who need help. Their need is not for counselling alone, but for a special service given in a personal way.

Another way in which the need for social work help arises is through the operation of the major, non-social work institutions of the welfare state. Whatever the organisational basis of social work, and whatever services it directly provides, it will be closely related to these institutions – the courts, the hospitals and other public agencies. Because it deals with human problems so closely connected with the fields of those other powerful institutions, social work cannot be entirely autonomous. Indeed, it cannot even always stop to make distinctions between those troubles, sorrows and adversities which are part of the human condition, and those which are created by the operation of these agencies. Its clients must include the casualties of others' cruelty and neglect, both public and private. The problem for social work is to achieve sufficient independence to act as an effective critic of other institutions, with a perceptible integrity of its own, able and willing to defend its clients' rights; yet also to be sufficiently involved in social policy to influence and put into practice improvements and reforms that will be of direct benefit to its clients.

Historically, the first social workers to become involved in the Welfare State's agencies took up positions which were a compromise between autonomy and involvement. Their role might be described as 'handmaidens' to the major institutions. Examples of this were probation officers ('servants of the courts') and both almoners and psychiatric social workers in the hospitals. They were originally employed by magistrates and doctors not so much to implement new programmes or provisions as to humanise and individualise the processes of these institutions. The appointment of probation officers allowed the courts to be less impersonal in dispensing justice; indeed it allowed them to take, through their officers, a personal interest in the post-court careers of some offenders who appeared before them. The appointment of almoners and psychiatric social workers enabled doctors to take some note of the wider context of their patients' lives, and hence let the hospital regime treat them rather more like people.

Most of my experience in social work has been in the court and the hospital setting. The problem of the 'handmaiden' role is the extent to which the social worker simply carries out the policies of the master agency in an uncritical way. If a court is unjust in its decisions, or if it bullies defendants, or bewilders them, or hurries through its business in a careless way, then its probation officers are as much involved in these cruel or disrespectful processes as any other officials. As a probation officer, I certainly felt deeply implicated and ashamed if any of these things occurred. Similarly, when I first went to work in a mental hospital, I was very conscious of my tacit collusion in decisions to treat patients by the use of drugs and ECT, processes I knew little about, but over which I felt concerned and suspicious. The social worker cannot dissociate himself from these aspects of the setting where he works. In so far as he is there when such decisions are made, or has contact with clients about whom they have been made, he is part of the process itself.

The defining characteristic of 'handmaiden' social work is that the really important decisions affecting clients are not made by the social worker, but by members of the master institution. It is usually right that this should be so. However imperfect the system of justice dispensed by courts, it is almost certainly better than would be dispensed by social workers, who have little legal training. Similarly, however suspect the practices of psychiatrists, they are qualified to treat the mentally ill, and social workers are not. However, the fact that others are the decision-makers should not allow social workers to shrug off their responsibility in the processes leading up to the decision, or after it. Probation officers often hide behind the power of the courts to evade difficult issues. In writing reports for the courts they 'respectfully suggest a certain course of action' when what they are really saying is that a man should go to prison; or they indicate a 'professional opinion that this young man will not respond to supervision' when they know the only real alternative open to the court is a sentence of borstal training. In this sort of way they preserve for themselves (but not for their clients) the illusion of being kind and liberal, and then sometimes even have the bad faith to criticise the harshness of courts which follow these tacit recommendations. This kind of self-deception is doubly dangerous, in that it contributes nothing to the humanisation of the court process, yet it disguises from the probation officer himself the extent to which he is as punitive and dismissive as (or in some cases more so than) the other officers of the court.

Equally, a probation officer who is genuinely convinced that non-custodial methods are more effective than traditional ones, yet who does not try to persuade and influence the court in each individual case, is really evading his responsibilities to his clients. In my own experience, courts will listen very carefully to good, logical arguments for any course of action, and will respect the sincerity of a probation officer who has the courage to show that he cares for his clients. In addition to this, probation officers have plenty of opportunities to prove that their methods work, both by keeping offenders under their supervision out of court, and through reporting back to case committees. In these ways they can build up credibility for their recommendations, however apparently contrary to tradition these may be. For example, because I had worked in a borstal before becoming a probation officer,

I was very doubtful of the value of long-term residential 'training' for young offenders, and this was reflected in my recommendations to courts. In my ten years in the probation service (five of these part-time), no approved school orders were made on any of the boys on whom I presented reports to court, only one fit person (care) order was made, and only two of my clients were sent to borstal. Allowing for the fact that this was in a mainly rural area, this still probably reflected a pattern of decisions by courts which was fairly strongly influenced away from long term residential training.

In the same way, the psychiatric setting allows social workers the opportunity to influence decisions about patients' treatment, so long as they are willing to take some responsibility for the consequences of those decisions. Where the social worker is seen as an outsider to the ward, who makes occasional forays from his office in another part of the hospital, his opinions are unlikely to be greatly heeded. Where he spends a good deal of time on the ward, is prepared to let nurses know and see how he works, shares in the day-to-day problems of handling difficult patients and identifies himself with the aims and ideals of the staff team, he is in a very strong position to recommend treatments which he himself will help to put into effect. Doctors, and especially consultants, are unlikely to have enough time to spend with patients to be specially confident that their diagnoses or prescriptions are the right ones, and where social workers and nurses can support each other in making clear and reasoned suggestions why another approach is likely to be more successful, they will probably be given the chance to make their ideas work. In my own experience, I found it much harder at first to speak out my opinions or hunches where the patient had been diagnosed as psychotic or where the problem directly concerned the prescription of drugs. I felt very anxious indeed the first time I suggested to the consultant psychiatrist that a client who had been diagnosed as a paranoid schizophrenic, and who had been discharged from hospital on a long-acting stabilising drug, would probably do much better if taken off the drug. I was both relieved and very anxious when my recommendation was accepted, and it was not until six months later, when my client was doing so well at his responsible job that he had been given promotion, that I felt any real confidence that I had been right.

In 'handmaiden' social work, the worker is in a semi-autonomous position, but answerable to decision makers from other professions. But in other forms of state social work, the worker is accountable through a local authority department to an elected committee. This is because the tasks done by local authority social workers are inextricably linked with residential homes, day care and various other domiciliary services. The tasks are not independent of these services and resources, but are concerned with how they are provided, and to whom. Thus the social worker is necessarily part of an organisation, and depends on others in it for the quality of help he offers. His job only makes sense within this organisational context.

The reason for this is that so many of the vulnerable people who come into contact with social workers need much more than the sort of help that can be given by one worker. There are children, handicapped people and the elderly frail who need residential care; mentally and physically ill people who need treatment; delinquents and others who need training; and many more who need special services in their homes. Many of the most delicate and difficult tasks of social work concern admitting people to residential establishments or providing appropriate services for complex needs. These tasks are not incidentals, but the very stuff of social work.

I hope I have not written this book in a way which suggests that social work is about 'solving' problems which arise from time to time in people's lives. In fact, the majority of clients face disadvantages and deprivations which are either very long-term or permanent. Children who have to come into care may need years of attention, love and consistency, to give them security until they become adults. The physically and mentally handicapped do not get better, and even with training are likely to need continual help of one kind or another. The chronically sick often face deterioration and loss of capacity. With such people, the social worker might ideally offer continuity and the sense of a concerned and realistic presence, sometimes outside the day-to-day process of helping, but always in touch with the overall picture and the whole person. His work would be as much to do with the client's sense of identity as with his social functioning.

In addition to these long term tasks which cannot be separated from residential and other services, there are the statutory social work tasks which were discussed in Chapter 4. Here again, the case for placing this work in a strong organisational context seems overwhelming. The tasks are unpleasant and difficult. They raise crucial issues about rights and obligations, both of the individuals concerned and of the state. They require a combination of sensitivity and soundness in distressing situations. In all these matters, there is a clear need for good supervision, public accountability, and a range of other services to back up the social worker. Since neither worker nor client enters particularly voluntarily into the relationship, supervision should focus the worker on his difficult task, helping him to stay open to the subtleties, yet enabling him to act decisively if this is required. But since what is always at stake is an admission of someone to a residential establishment of one kind or another, and legal powers to compel it, the worker's position in that organisational network is important. Both his legal powers and his role as part of the agency need to be clear to the clients.

In statutory work, neither the social worker nor his department can select their clients, and usually the client has not chosen them or asked for their help either. But because the department has many resources, including residential facilities, it can offer something even to the most desperate and destructive people. Thus the social worker can persist even when there are no quick cures or easy solutions. As part of a diverse and resourceful organisation, he can stick with clients that he could not possibly help on his own.

Before the reorganisation of local authority social work in 1970, the services I have been describing were fragmented between a number of departments. The children's department had started with a clear but limited function – caring for children deprived of family life – and had broadened its scope to include juvenile delinquency and preventive work with families. The welfare department had different traditions in its care for and work with the elderly. Other services were scattered in health and education departments. There were strong arguments for unifying all these services and strengthening their organisation. The old divisions of tasks created overlaps, gaps and anomalies. A single department could take an overview of community needs, plan and deploy resources according to its research findings. It could strive to abolish unjust variations in provision, to make rational decisions about priorities. The greater political muscle of a large department could be used to win more resources for client groups. Then there could be developed a more flexible approach to problems, using a range of responses – from material aid to residential care – in the most constructive combination.

The difficulty since 1970 has been in sustaining good face-to-face work with clients in this new kind of organisation. Because of its size and complexity, the social services department tended to emphasise administrative efficiency, and consequently to reward precision, numeracy, paperwork and the observance of agency procedures. The individual responsibility and personal commitment which were necessary for good work with clients were too small-scale and hard to quantify to be properly valued in the early days after reorganisation. There was a tension between organisational goals and professional standards, with the result that social workers either moved into managerial positions in an attempt to influence policy, or became so frustrated that they sabotaged well-intentioned management initiatives.

Another unforeseen problem was that the wide range of benefits and services available from the new department gave rise to confusion about its function. Neither clients nor referral agents understood its powers or limits. A flood of problems, both trivial and chronic, descended upon it. Managers claimed that the rise (about 15 per cent more referrals each year) reflected a growing awareness among the public of their rights to services. Social workers felt that they were being bombarded by people whose expectations of what they could do were often quite unreasonable. Their work became less about the positive identification of need, and more about the rationing of scarce resources, and especially of the personal attention they could pay their clients.

The fundamental ambiguity about the social services department has been whether it was primarily providing personal services, or concerned with more impersonal processes of allocating various kinds of assistance. Inevitably, the management structure laid more emphasis on the services it could measure, cost, quantify and control. Politically and administratively, the expansion of services was the expansion of expenditure on aids and adaptations, telephones and other forms of material aid, and on new building programmes for day and residential care. Yet in relation to these developments, social workers have seen themselves merely as form-fillers and assessors, giving (or more often withholding) what was requested by applicants. Instead of using resources for creative purposes, taking imaginative initiatives to improve the quality of people's lives, they were required to conduct hurried investigations of hundreds of applications and issue departmental decisions, made on impersonal criteria. Since the social services department also dealt in discretionary assistance to very needy people, who had failed to establish titles to other, less stigmatised benefits, some of their work took on the characteristics of public assistance. Thus a combination of factors has gradually altered the style and flavour of local authority social work, shifting it away from the personal and towards a more procedural, official approach. This has even influenced the way traditional social work tasks have been performed, placing emphasis on moving clients around or giving them things rather than listening to what they think and sharing their feelings.

As a result of all these developments, social workers became less confident in their approach to many of the more complex and demanding aspects of their work. With the ending of the old specialisms, most of the experienced workers were promoted to advisory and supervisory posts. The sheer size and complexity of the organisation prevented them from giving effective day-to-day support to less experienced staff, and procedural rules of thumb were no substitute for detailed supervision in depth in these areas of work. Insecurity was also created by the loss of a sense of where professional boundaries with other services were to be drawn. Almost anything and everything seemed to be the business of social work, and an anxious feeling of unmanageably wide responsibility was not conducive to the clear focus required by these subtle and complicated problems. Finally, public criticism put social workers even more on the defensive, especially in cases of alleged ill-treatment to children. Their anxiety made it harder to find the balance between extremes of under and over-reaction which is so essential in these cases.

Both as a result of this loss of confidence and as a factor contributing to it, social workers have been less successful in recent years in demonstrating the effectiveness of their involvement on a large scale in social problems. The 1960s had been a period of optimistic expansion, in which new policies were pioneered with apparent success. It was one of the strongest arguments for the creation of a larger, more powerful, social services department that it would give social workers a more decisive say in important matters affecting their clients' welfare. They had come to feel that in situations of crisis, where their clients needed official help, crucial decisions were usually made by members of other organisations – the courts, the police, the Supplementary Benefits Commission, the housing department or the health authorities. These institutions had great power over their clients, but did not always seem to treat them respectfully, or understand them as social workers did. Thus although the 1970 Act itself gave social workers no new powers, it seemed the culmination of a number of trends in policy and administration – earlier referrals of problems of debt, family break-up, eviction, and the provisions of the 1969 Act in relation to delinquency – which gave them more opportunities to influence decisions crucial to the future pattern of clients' lives.

Yet none of these new initiatives seemed to bear fruit. An enormous increase in interventions in families did not stem a rising tide of child abuse. Care orders in relation to this problem increased from 2,957 in 1972 to 4,701 in 1974-5. The total number of children in care rose higher than ever, and the proportion of ordinary (non-delinquent) children in foster homes dropped lower than at any time since the early 1950s. The number of children in prisons, borstals, detention centres and secure units reached the highest level since the First World War. In 1969 there had been only 300 boys under seventeen in borstal; by 1976 there were 1600. Another 6000 were in junior detention centres. Whereas there had been virtually no secure provision in the old approved school system before 1962, by 1974 there was an estimated need for 600 secure places for children on care orders. To try to deal with these problems, social workers had largely withdrawn from work in community mental health that had been developing before 1970, and standards in work with the elderly and handicapped were also declining. Even taking account of many adverse social trends during this period, it was a very discouraging record.

One reaction among social workers to these failures was to blame them all onto the organisational changes which had taken place in 1970. They blamed the unwieldy size of the department for poor communications and a bureaucratic style of administration. They pointed out that bad management was responsible for much of the overwhelming pressure on them from inappropriate referrals. They drew attention to a fall in the standard of supervision which resulted from attempts by the hierarchy to 'monitor' large numbers of difficult cases, to exercise a form of remote control over them which undermined them when they most needed support. They blamed organisational interference and muddle for their sense of lost autonomy and professional responsibility, and for low morale.

The most extreme expression of these views took the form of an assertion that 'it is no longer possible to do real social work or give real help in a social services department'. Some disillusioned social workers have argued that the whole social work task should somehow be taken out of this department and given a separate one of its own. Others have suggested a separation of social work from the statutory functions of the local authority. Others still have argued that all work involving personal relationships should be handed over to voluntary bodies; and some are making the same point with their feet, by deserting social services for jobs in independent organisations.

This is particularly dangerous because, with the unification of all the local authority agencies, the social services department has a virtual monopoly of state personal services. Its standards determine the quality of life of the 50,000 children who come into public care in any year; of the 40,000 who enter local authority old people's homes; and the many more who rely on its day care and domiciliary services. It is impossible to imagine voluntary agencies achieving a coverage of the country which would allow them to provide services on anything like this scale. Only state services could hope to achieve an acceptable uniformity and geographical distribution of facilities to meet these massive needs.

Indeed, for all the characteristic weaknesses of the large-scale social services departments, voluntary agencies have not been without their different faults. While some have chosen to work with people who are among the most difficult in any statutory social worker's caseload – ex-prisoners, chronic mental patients, cripples or multi-problem families – others have insisted that their specialism requires very rigorous selection procedures, and choose only clients who suit their methods. There are strong arguments for this kind of specialisation for the development of new techniques, of new standards of excellence, and for purposes of research. But such selectivity always relies ultimately on a state system to deal with its rejects, who are often among the most urgently or chronically needy. Thus modern voluntary agencies sometimes share a weakness with their historical ancestors, the Victorian charitable foundations. Just as the earliest social workers did not hesitate to reject or pass on to the Poor Law authorities those they considered 'undeserving' or 'unhelpable', so today some voluntary bodies develop their own lines of treatment or care according to their own priorities, secure in the knowledge that the state will provide, by its own standards (whatever these may be) for the rest.

I do not want to underestimate the contribution of voluntary agencies in recent years both to new methods and to the preservation of old values and standards. They can be small in scale, informal and democratic in style. Their offices can be more open and welcoming places, comfortable for meetings and group activities. They can be participatory in their approach, and break down traditional demarcations of roles, giving clients responsibility for day-to-day and policy decisions. Transition from client to worker roles can be made easier in the absence of public accountability. They can be flexible in their methods, moving easily between individual, family, group and community work. In all these ways they can give an example and a lead which statutory agencies can follow. But they remain outside the organisational framework of collective responsibility for social problems represented by the state's institutions. Voluntary agencies have sometimes been known to become esoteric, self-indulgent and precious – irrelevant to the key issues of social policy. Few reforms of state services can be traced directly to their social workers, who in the past have even opposed advances in state provision. None of these historical weaknesses give good grounds for reducing the role of voluntary agencies, but nor do they encourage total reliance on them for the future role of social work in a welfare state.

Because of the key position of social services departments in British social work, I believe it should be the primary aim of social workers to improve standards of work in these departments. Criticisms should be aimed at raising their level of practice, not at bringing about their downfall. For all their organisational faults, they still embody a potential for giving real help to their clients. The legislative framework which underpins social work is still fundamentally the same as before 1970, and is basically sound. If social workers can return to their first principles and can hang on to what is best in their traditions, there is no overwhelming reason why standards should not begin to rise again. Indeed, I think there is evidence that they have already begun to do so.

In order that this should continue, I believe that three organisational changes should be resisted. The first is a further change of departmental boundaries which could make the social services department responsible for still more material benefits not directly connected with the personal and social problems it already tackles. There are signs that politicians and administrators are keen to get social workers to do the discretionary work of supplementary benefits. But there are also indications that social workers and their managers are resisting this, and may be able to influence policy against this pressure. Second, the growth of a private sector in social work should be restricted. The American example shows that where fee-paying social work help becomes available on a large scale to middle-class consumers, the state services are starved of trained workers and other resources, and become impoverished, low status agencies with poor standards of practice. Third, any trend which takes qualified and experienced workers away from face-to-face dealings with clients in the most difficult social work tasks (especially statutory work) should be resisted. Here the Australian example is relevant. In Australia, most statutory work is done by untrained or less qualified 'welfare officers', while the higher status and more fully trained 'social workers' are employed in more remote consultative or therapeutic posts. Services, and especially residential care, are consequently at a primitive level of development more akin to the British situation before the legislative and administrative changes of 1948.

I do not wish to imply that the quality of helping in British social work can be improved simply by 'holding the line', or trying to restore the *status quo* before 1970. The whole situation has changed, and a much more active and forward-looking approach is required. The expansionist policies of the 1960s had already led social work into far more complex and politically dangerous territories than it had entered before; the creation of the unified department merely concentrated all the problems and contradictions of these developments into one agency, and focused the public's attention upon it. What was more, the social services department entered the politics of welfare as a major force just when the tide of public opinion was turning against recipients of welfare provision. On the defensive, social workers argued their case far less impressively than they had in the more favourable climate of the 1960s. What is now needed, and what has begun to emerge, is a more positive and constructive approach to the policy dilemmas of present-day social services work.

The basis for this new approach is a very penetrative and self-critical examination of all the work that the department does. Two factors have begun to contribute to such a day-to-day analysis and response. The first is teamwork. Immediately after 1970, when all social workers were placed in 'teams' and each worker was given a generic caseload, this was a doubtful boon. Insecurity often made team members either competitive or protective, so that standards fell as expertise was not shared. Now colleagues are beginning to give each other real help, and hold each other to the most difficult tasks, including sharing responsibility for the toughest cases, and accompanying each other on frightening visits. But in addition to this invaluable help in casework social workers can get together to analyse the overall picture their work presents, the strengths and weaknesses of their joint approaches to problems, and the appropriateness or otherwise of their department's response to the problems presented to it. This has contributed to a re-emergence of specialisation, both by individual aptitude and by teams, and to a more rational and economic use of social workers' skills.

The second factor which has helped this constructive approach has been the growth of intake teams. Initially this was mainly a response to the sense of bombardment, often with inappropriate referrals, that all social workers felt after 1970. Intake workers represented a screening process for referrals, and a defence for other workers with large numbers of difficult long-term cases. Then intake teams started to specialise in identification of and work with referrals that could be most constructively helped on a short-term basis. This in turn required an analysis of methods of helping, and an attempt to develop a short-term approach which was purposeful but which, by use of the notion of 'contracts', took full account of the client's view of his problem. It necessitated discussing more fully with clients what help could be given, and how, so that the limitations as well as the potentialities of the department could be made explicit. This also gave the client a chance to express his hopes and fears about the help he was requesting.

At first this approach was applied in a very rough-and-ready way, and many mistakes were made. Some teams used the notions of short-term work and contracts inappropriately, as a way of rationing resources and limiting the offer of help. They seemed to become unable to listen to clients or to let them get to the worst in their circumstances, especially if this might entail the worker being asked for something more than practical assistance. But now there is evidence of a far more imaginative approach to intake work in many areas. Teams are finding time to question their own methods, and their key position as doorkeepers to the agency gives them opportunities to identify new trends in referrals, and to plan and carry out new initiatives.

What seems to be needed is an extension into teamwork of the self-awareness and self-criticism that I have tried to suggest as appropriate for individual social workers in the rest of this book. By continually asking, 'What are we doing?' and 'Why did we do that?', teams can reach a similar state of awareness of their responses to pressures (from referral agents and clients), and can find ways of using these constructively. They also have the advantage of being able to use each other in reaching this awareness, and having the opportunity to hold each other to the task of sharing it with clients in whatever way seems most helpful.

A few examples I have heard from one intake team may illustrate this point. The group have several times identified clusters of similar referrals where the action required of the social worker was of no possible help to the client, but simply a way of allaying the anxieties or the consciences of the referral agents – usually from another official body. As a policy, therefore, the team decided to point this out to the referral agents in all future cases of this type, rather than to continue going through the motions of a pointless exercise. Second, the group became aware of its own need to 'solve' problems, or at least to persuade itself that it was doing something constructive about any referral it accepted. This 'production ethos' could lead to a kind of collective myth about the team's potency and effectiveness which made it hard for individuals to admit to themselves or their clients when they had failed. Third, and linked, the group recognised that they were constantly refusing to take up referrals of cases where there was no evidence that social work help could produce change. While there were grounds for turning away many such referrals, others were of people who needed the presence of a concerned helper to make their life bearable, even if he could not make it better. They therefore decided to try to offer (or persuade colleagues in long-term teams to offer) some kind of service to such people, who had been neglected since the services had been reorganised.

All these developments might well, of course, have been instigated through management and supervision rather than through teamwork, and no doubt in many areas they have occurred in this way. The point here is that when social workers do not feel they are getting the benefit of good management or supervision, they can achieve a great deal on their own, and can then enter into a constructive dialogue with managers and seniors about the initiatives they propose. While this has proved difficult in some authorities (because of managerial insecurity and suspicion), where social workers can form strong and united teams these problems seem greatly reduced.

Another encouraging development has been the growing awareness at all levels of the social services departments of the importance of small-scale and local responses to local needs. In 1970, administrative changes vested considerable power in the chief executives and their management teams. Strong central control was seen as a prerequisite for rational planning. Research departments at headquarters were to provide the data for an overview of the whole community, and top management were to standardise services and promote territorial justice. Now it is being recognised that this undermined morale and initiative at the local level, and that the provision of services for specially vulnerable people often defied operations on the scale of large organisations. Even research is now increasingly and beneficially looking at the local level and the detailed personal processes of helping.

However, some wider problems still remain, and are common to most areas. Because of the role of social services departments as generalised welfare agencies for the most deprived sector of society – and hence of its strong undertones of public assistance under the Poor Law – the status of their clients is a highly undesirable one in terms of civil rights. Many people referred to social services are in a state of limbo, having failed to establish a clear title to benefits or services from the major institutions of social welfare. They have been referred by doctors, teachers, social security officers or housing managers who find them too difficult and troublesome to heal, teach, assist or house. Often they represent the failures of those institutions to meet urgent or exceptional needs. For social workers meekly to accept them as clients is often to ensure that they lose their rights to those benefits and services, and get instead a less appropriate, inferior or harsher provision from their own agency. Mr and Mrs Miller and their daughter Shirley seemed to be an example of this. The present situation therefore demands from social workers a vigorous assertion of potential clients' rights to decent services from the major institutions of the Welfare State.

It may well be realistic today to see each new application or referral to a social services department as potentially a case of jeopardised citizenship. In becoming clients, people may be in danger of having their civil and social rights undermined, eroded or usurped. Respect for persons, as the first principle of social work, seems to me to demand that the social worker defends the rights of his clients and potential clients as if they were his own, or those of a member of his family. This may well mean that much of his time is spent in advocacy and other welfare rights activity which would not, in a juster world, be a major part of the social worker's task. Another part of his work may be concerned with being a watchdog for injustice in his own department – for the kind of expediency, high-handedness or paternalism that makes clients more helpless than they were before the department's intervention. These wrongs cannot be righted by individual integrity alone; they require the collective action of social workers united in an agreed opposition to policies and methods which they have experienced as undermining their clients.

In the late 1960s and early 1970s there was an unfortunate tendency for social workers to think in terms of a dichotomy between the professional and the political. At its crudest, the split was conveyed in the 'radical' notion that casework was a social sedative, and the 'traditional' idea that it was unprofessional to proclaim political opinions. Changes in social policy and administration have made social work a more political activity, and have given social workers more political sophistication. But ultimately the confidence to argue for a constructive programme for change must rest on the good quality of its work in professional tasks. As social workers begin to rediscover their faith in themselves as helpers, they may also once again find their courage and their voices. Instead of using much of their energy resisting their organisations, they may find ways of uniting with their managers to demand a better life for their clients.